SWU-800-009

UNIFORMS OF RUSSIAN ARMY DURING THE YEARS 1825-1855 VOL. 9

UNDER THE REIGN OF NICHOLAS I
EMPEROR OF RUSSIA BETWEEN 1825 TO 1855
GUARDS SAPPER. ENGINEERS, STAFF & OTHERS

From the Viskovatov's greatest work:
"Historical description of the clothing and
arms of the Russian Army"

English translation by Mark Conrad

SOLDIERSHOP PUBLISHING

AUTHOR
Aleksandr Vasilevich Viskovatov born 22 April (4 May New Style) 1804, died 27 February (11 March) 1858 in St. Petersburg, Russian military historian. He graduated from the 1st Cadet Corps and served in the artillery, the hydrographic depot of the Naval Ministry, and then in the Department of Military Educational Institutions. He mainly studied historical artifacts and the histories of military units. Viskovatov's greatest work was the Historical Description of the Clothing and Arms of the Russian Army.

PUBLISHING'S NOTE
None of **unpublished** images or text of our book may be reproduced in any format without the expressed written permission of Soldiershop.com when not indicate as marked with license creative commons 3.0 or 4.0. The publisher remains to disposition of the possible having right for all the doubtful sources images or not identifies. Our trademark: Soldiershop Publishing ©, The names of our series: Soldiers&Weapons, Battlefield, War in colour, PaperSoldiers, Soldiershop e-book etc. are herein © by Soldiershop.com.

NOTE ABOUT BOOK PRINTING BEFORE 1925
This book may contain text or images coming from a reproduction of a book published before 1925 (over seventy years ago). No effort has been made to modernize or standardize the spelling used in the original text, so this book may have occasional imperfections such as missing or blurred pages, poor pictures, errant marks, etc. that were either part of the original artifact, or were introduced by the scanning process. We believe this work is culturally important, and despite the imperfections, have elected to bring it back into print (digital and/or paper) as part of our continuing commitment to the preservation of printed works worldwide. We appreciate your understanding of the imperfections in the preservation process, and hope you enjoy this valuable book. Now this book is purpose re-built and is proof-read and re-type set from the original to provide an outstanding experience of reflowing text, also for an ebook reader. However Soldiershop publishing added, enriched, revised and overhauled the text, images, etc. of the cover and the book. Therefore, the job is now to all intents and purposes a derivative work, and the added, new and original parts of the book are the copyright of Soldiershop. On this second unpublished part of the book none of images or text may be reproduced in any format without the expressed written permission of Soldiershop. Almost many of the images of our books and prints are taken from original first edition prints or books that are no longer in copyright and are therefore public domain. We have been a specialized bookstore for a long time so we (and several friends antiquarian booksellers) have readily available a lot of ancient, historical and illustrated books not in copyright. Each of our prints, art designs or illustrations is either our own creation, or a fully digitally restoration by our computer artists, or non copyrighted images. All of our prints are "tagged" with a registered digital copyright. Soldiershop remains to disposition of the possible having right for all the doubtful sources images or not identifies.

LICENSES COMMONS
Much of the text in this book are from the *"Memoirs of the Empress Catherine II., by Catherine II, Empress of Russia"* This book is for the use of anyone anywhere at no cost and with almost no restrictions whatsoever. You may copy it, give it away or re-use it under the terms of the similar creative commons License. This book may utilize material marked with license creative commons 3.0 or 4.0 (CC BY 4.0), (CC BY-ND 4.0), (CC BY-SA 4.0) or (CC0 1.0). We give appropriate attribution credit and indicate if change were made below in the acknowledgements field.

ACKNOWLEDGEMENTS
A Special Thanks to NYPL and other institutions for their kindly permission to use some images of his archives, collections or books used in our book.

Title: **UNIFORMS OF RUSSIAN ARMY DURING THE YEARS 1825-1855. VOL. 9** -Under the reign of Nicholas I emperor of Russia between 1825-1855
By A.V.Viskovatov. Serie edit by Luca S. Cristini. First edition by Soldiershop. April 2019
Cover & Art Design: Luca S. Cristini. Plates re-colorations by Anna Cristini. ISBN code: 978-88-93274265
Published by Luca Cristini Editore, via Orio 35/4- 24050 Zanica (BG) ITALY. www.soldiershop.com

UNIFORMS OF THE RUSSIAN ARMY DURING THE YEARS 1825-1855 VOL. 9

UNDER THE REIGN OF NICHOLAS I EMPEROUR OF RUSSIA BETWEEN 1825 AND 1855

*

GUARDS SAPPER, ENGINEERS, STAFF & OTHERS

Portrait of the Emperor Nicholas I 1856 by George Dawe (c.1828, Helsinki University)

HISTORICAL DESCRIPTION OF THE CLOTHING AND ARMS OF THE RUSSIAN ARMY - A.V. VISKOVATOV
(First English translation by Mark Conrad)

Soldiershop is glad to presents the complete collection of the great job made by A.V. Viskovatov dedicated to the uniforms and weapons belonging from the first Zar and Russian emperors to the Russian army during the Napoleonic period, until 1860 about. The time we considered in this volume corresponds to the reigns of Nicholas I that was the Emperor of Russia from 1825 until 1855. He was also the King of Poland and Grand Duke of Finland. He is best known as a political conservative whose reign was marked by geographical expansion, repression of dissent, economic stagnation, poor administrative policies, a corrupt bureaucracy, and frequent wars that culminated in Russia's defeat in the Crimean War of 1853–56.

Our reprint in based on the original 19th century volumes. This part is distributed at now on six volumes.

Our new edition, the first ever published in English, both on paper and digital format, boasts a large number of color plates, many of them unpublished and re-coloured by our team of expert artists and scholars of uniformology. Each volume is based on 100 color plates or more, always accompanied by the original translated text which describes the subjects of the plates.

A unique work in its genre, a must have in any respecting collection!

Aleksandr Vasilevich Viskovatov born 22 April (4 May New Style) 1804, died 27 February (11 March) 1858 in St. Petersburg, Russian military historian. He graduated from the 1st Cadet Corps and served in the artillery, the hydrographic depot of the Naval Ministry, and then in the Department of Military Educational Institutions.

He mainly studied historical artifacts and the histories of military units. Viskovatov's greatest work was the Historical Description of the Clothing and Arms of the Russian Army (Vols. 1-30, St. Petersburg, 1841-62; 2nd ed. Vols. 1-34, St. Petersburg - Novosibirsk - Leningrad, 1899-1948). This work is based on a great quantity of archival documents and contains four thousand colored illustrations.

Viskovatov was the author of Chronicles of the Russian Army (Books 1-20, St. Petersburg, 1834-42) and Chronicles of the Russian Imperial Army (Parts 1-7, St. Petersburg, 1852). He collected valuable material on the history of the Russian navy which went into A Short Overview of Russian Naval Campaigns and General Voyages to the End of the XVII Century (St. Petersburg, 1864; 2nd edition Moscow, 1946). Together with A.I. Mikhailovskii-Danilevskii he helped prepare and create the Military Gallery in the Winter Palace.

He wrote the historical military inscriptions for the walls of the Hall of St. George in the Great Palace of the Kremlin. (From the article in the Soviet Military Encyclopedia.)

CONTENTS
*
Preface pag. 5

45 - Life Guards Sapper Battalion. Pag. 7

46 - Life Guards Horse Pioneer Squadron. Pag. 9

47 - Guards Engineers. Pag. 11

48 - Guards General Staff. Pag. 12

49 - Guards Garrison battalion. Pag. 13

50 - Guards Invalid Companies. Pag. 15

51 - Guards Equipage. Pag. 16

52 - Instructional Troops. Pag. 18
*
Notes pag. 26

Plates pag. 31

HISTORICAL DESCRIPTION OF THE CLOTHING AND ARMS OF THE RUSSIAN ARMY
Guards Sapper, Engineers, Staff & others 1825-1855

CHANGES IN THE UNIFORMS AND EQUIPMENT OF TEMPORARY FORCES FROM 1801 TO 1825.

XLV. LIFE-GUARDS SAPPER BATTALION. [*Leib-Gvardii Sapernyi batalion.*]

11 February 1826 – Company-grade officers' grey riding-trousers and dark-green pants with high boots, and the lower ranks' pants with gaiters [*kragi*], were replaced with long dark-green **pants** with red piping down the side seams. Underneath these pants and over the boots, lower ranks at all times, but company-grade officers when in formation or at any time when wearing the sash, were to wear black cloth **half-gaiters** [*polushtiblety*] buttoned with five or six small buttons the same color as the coat buttons. Generals, field-grade officers, and adjutants wearing these pants, the same as for company-grade officers with troop units, were ordered to not wear gaiters, but have boots with the **spurs** driven in. Along with these changes, the horizontal belt for the **knapsack** was ordered to be worn under the lower coat buttons, and the greatcoat was to be rolled into a tube inside a special oilskin case made of raven's-duck (Illus. 796). Clerks and in general all noncombatant lower ranks were ordered to wear gray riding trousers without wide stripes [1].

10 May 1826 - Generals, field-grade officers, and those company-grade officers who were mounted when in formation, were during the summer ordered to wear white linen **pants** without integral spats [*kozyrki*], of the same pattern as the dark-green ones (Illus. 797). Instead of the linen pants, they were also allowed to wear suede pants of the same pattern [2].

15 September 1826 – For lower ranks who served out the regulation number of years without reproach and instead of exercising their right to retirement voluntarily remained on service were ordered to wear an additional **gold galloon** stripe on the left sleeve, above the yellow tape established on 29 March 1825 [3].

12 December 1826 – Officers' épées [*shpagi*] were replaced by **half-sabers** [*polusabli*] of the same pattern as introduced on 20 August 1830 for Army infantry and described above (see Grenadier regiments) (Illus. 797) [4].

1 January 1827 - Small forged and stamped stars on officers' epaulettes were established to distinguish **rank**, of the same appearance and according to the same scheme as for other troops described above [5].

14 February 1827 – The **pocket flaps** of officers' coats were not to have red piping [6].

31 July 1827 – Numbers and letters on the **covers for shakos and cartridge pouches**, instead of being made from yellow cloth, were ordered to be painted in yellow oilpaint [7].

19 November 1827 - On coats and greatcoats, the lower edge of the **collar** was to have red cloth piping [8].

14 December 1827 - The **lace** [*nashivka*] sewn onto lower ranks' left sleeves, instituted on 15 September 1826, was ordered to be silver non-commissioned officers' galloon [9].

24 March 1828 - The **coats** of lower ranks were not to be tailored with cinches [10].

24 April 1828 – All combatant lower ranks in the battalion were given new-pattern **shakos**, identical to those introduced for the preceding Guards Infantry regiments, i.e. taller than before, without leather trim on the sides, with white cord around the top edge, and with the previous pompons. The shako plate, in connection with the shako's increased height, was also to be of a new, slightly altered pattern, made from white tine as before (Illus. 798). Along with this the following additional changes were introduced:

1.) The width of **crossbelts** and **swordbelts** was stipulated to be 2 vershoks [3-1/2 inches]; that of knapsack shoulder straps—1-1/2 vershoks [2 5/8 inches]; and of the strap across the chest—1-1/8 vershoks [2 inches].

2.) **Knapsacks** were to be of calfskin as before but with black leather trim. The knapsack was prescribed to be 9 vershoks [15-3/4 inches] broad, 8 vershoks [14 inches] high, and 2-1/2 vershoks [4-3/8 inches] wide. From the upper edge the length of the cover was 6 vershoks [10 1/2 inches].

3.) All non-combatant personnel of non-commissioned officer rank were given dark-green **frock coats** [*syurtuki*] with a single row of buttons to replace their grey coats [*mundiry*] now in use. The frock coats had the same collar, cuffs, and shoulder straps as for combatant personnel. Pants were the previous grey with red piping on the side seams.

4.) Non-combatant craftsmen of the lower ranks, as well as medical orderlies, were to wear grey cloth **jackets** [*kurtki*] modeled on the previous coat. Pants were to be as for the non-combatants above [11].

18 May 1829 – Non-commissioned officers put forward by the high command for promotion to officers by virtue of years of service were allowed to wear silver **sword knots** [12].

16 December 1829 - The black cuffs of officers' **frock coats** were changed to dark green, with red piping as before [13].

26 December 1829 - All ranks were ordered to have uniform **buttons** with the raised image of the two-headed eagle prescribed for the shako plate [14].

8 June 1832 - Officers were permitted to wear **moustaches** [15].

3 January 1833 – Cloth **half-gaiters** were abolished for company-grade officers and lower ranks, and **sword knots** were ordered to be kept only by those non-commissioned officers who had received them in silver [16].

20 February 1833 - All combatant ranks were given a new-pattern summer **pants** or **trousers** [*pantalony ili bryuki*] without buttons or integral spats (Illus. 799) [17].

22 February 1833 -. Field and Company-grade officers who had to be mounted when in formation were permitted to have **horses** with long tails [18].

28 March 1834 – Confirmation was given to a new pattern of **short-sword** [*tesak*] with yellow brass mountings and a straight blade, identical to that introduced at this time in the Guards Foot Artillery (Illus. 800) [19].

26 September 1834 - Lower ranks were directed to wear the **knapsack** on two belts lying crosswise over the chest (Illus. 801) [20].

20 August 1835 - Officers were directed to wear the **knapsack** using only two lacquered shoulder belts; there were to be no straps that cross over the front of the body or the chest. For lower ranks a linen case or pocket for the forage cap was to be put on the outside of the knapsack on the side that lay on the soldier's back. These cases were to be made from the linings of worn-out coats. For drummers the knapsack was worn over the shoulder on one belt as before, worn over the left shoulder [21].

31 January 1836 - The lower ranks' **greatcoat** was to have nine buttons instead of ten: six down the front, two on the shoulder straps, and one on the flaps behind [22].

27 April 1836 - **Lower pompons** [*repeiki*] were to be lined with black leather [23].

13 May 1836 - Girths for officers' **saddles** were to be dark green with red stripes [24].

14 January 1837 - Handles of **entrenching tools** were to have the wooden parts varnished instead of painted with oil paints, and the same directives for the fitting and carrying of these tools applied as described above (see Grenadier regiments) [25].

15 June 1837 - Approval was given to the new pattern of officers' **sash**, identical with that introduced at this time for the preceding troops and described above [26].

17 December 1837 - Approval was given to a new pattern of officers' **epaulettes** identical to that introduced at this time for the preceding troops, i.e. with the addition of a fourth twist of braid [27].

17 January 1838 – The **battalion staff-bugler** [*shtab-gornist*], who during summer had to be mounted when in formation, was ordered to wear winter pants, and instead of a knapsack—a cavalry pattern valise. His horse was to have its bridle and saddle of the patterns for mounted artillerymen, without a shabrack or saddlecloth [28].

4 January 1839 - Officers were not to have any bows or bands on the front of their **pants** or **trousers**. These were to be worn completely plain in the manner prescribed for lower ranks [29].

16 March 1839 - Lower ranks' **swordbelts** were to be 1-1/2 vershoks [2-3/5 inches] wide, while drummers' **crossbelts** were 2-1/2 vershoks [4-2/5 inches] wide, as before [30].

16 October 1840 - A regulation was confirmed concerning sewn-on **silver galloon** or **chevrons** for lower ranks, as laid out above (see Guards Lancer regiments [31].

23 January 1841 - The capes of officers' **greatcoats** were to be 1 arshin [28 inches] long as measured from the lower edge of the collar [32].

8 April 1843 - A new pattern **shako** curving inward at the bottom was approved, identical to that confirmed at this time for Guards infantry, cavalry, and artillery (Illus. 802). Also established was trimming on the **shoulder straps** of sergeants [*feldfebeli*], non-commissioned officers [*unter-ofitsery*], and lance-corporals [*yefreitory*], following the same scheme as for Army sapper battalions, but with army galloon changed to Guards tape [*gvardeiskii bason*]. On this same date, in order to be more easily distinguished from generals' epaulettes, it was directed that **drum-majors' epaulettes** have red silk between the braided gold threads and in the hanging fringe [33].

10 May 1843 - Cover flaps [*kryshki*] for **cartridge pouches**, sewn to the box, were to be: 4-3/4 vershoks [8-3/8 inches] long, 5 vershoks [8-3/4 inches] wide at the top edge, and 5-6/8 vershoks [9-7/8 inches] wide along the bottom edge [34].

2 January 1844 - Officers were to have a **cockade** on the cap band of the forage cap, identical with that introduced at this time for the preceding troops and described above (see Grenadier regiments) [35].

9 May 1844 - Shakos were replaced by **helmets** of black lacquered leather, with two visors, metal appointments the same color as the buttons, and plumes—red horse hair for musicans and black for other ranks, with the previous plate, all identical to the pattern introduced for Guards infantry, cavalry, and artillery (Illus. 803) [36].

20 May 1844 - Based on the new general scheme for lower ranks' **forage caps**, the piping around the top and along both edges of the band was to be red, the band was to be black plissé, with cut-outs backed by yellow cloth: in the 1st Sapper Company—Cyrillic 1.S.R., in the 1st Miner Company—Cyrillic 1.M.R., and so on. Officers' cap bands were velvet, without numbers or letters, as before [37].

17 November 1844 - Instructions for storing and protecting the **helmet plume** [*kasochnyi sultan*] were approved, as related above in detail (see Grenadier regiments) [38].

4 January 1845 - Officers' helmets were to have a **cockade** on the right side, identical to that instruduced for the preceding troops and described above (see Grenadier regiments) (Illus. 804) [39].

9 August 1845 - In camp dress [*lagernaya forma*] **helmets** were ordered to be worn without plumes, even if personnel entitled to them were wearing dress coats [*mundiry*] (Illus. 804) [40].

23 June 1846 - Approval was given to a description of the **firing-cap pouch** (see Grenadier regiments) [41].

19 May 1847 – Noncombatant lower ranks were given gray **forage caps** (see Guards heavy infantry regiments) [42].

29 November 1847 – Officer candidates and distinguished officer candidates [*Yunkery i portupei-praporshchiki*] carrying out the duties of commissioned officers were to wear officers' **half-sabers** [*polusabli*] instead of short swords [*tesaki*] (see Guards infantry regiments) [43].

9 January 1848 - On those days when they were obliged to remain in ceremonial dress after the mounting of the guard, field and company-grade officers were permitted for walking-out to wear the **frock coat** with **helmet** and **plume** [44].

19 April 1849 - Approval was given to the method of fitting a belt to English signal bugles (see Grenadier regiments) [45].

14 September 1849 - A pattern of **percussion pistol** for officers was confirmed (see Grenadier regiments) [46].

9 and 25 November 1849 - Approval was given to a method of fitting the **helmet** (see Grenadier regiments) [47].

24 December 1849 - The grip of the hilt of the **gold half-saber** awarded for bravery was to be gold [48].

17 January 1851 - Approval was given to descriptions for folding up and turning back the skirts of soldiers' **greatcoats** (see Grenadier regiments) [49].

8 July 1851 - Gun-lock covers [*polunagalishcha*] were abolished and approval given to descriptions of the **drum**, **water flask**, and other items (see Guards heavy infantry regiments) [50].

20 October 1851 - A list and description of items to be carried by the soldier in his **knapsack** while on the march and during inspections was confirmed (see Grenadier regiments) [51].

26 January 1852 - The gray cloth **forage caps** of noncombatant lower ranks were to have bands of the same color as the collar of combatant personnel [52].

28 December 1852 – **Undress shabracks** [*vitse-chepraki*] for campaign dress were approved, of the pattern established for Guards foot artillery [53].

3 January 1853 - **Frock coats** of non-combatant lower ranks were prescribed to reach to the lower part of the knee [54].

18 February 1854 – Field and company-grade officers and adjutants, when in formation, were to have a valise on their **saddle** (see Grenadier regiments) [55].

29 April 1854 - Campaign **greatcoats** were approved for officers (see Grenadier regiments) [56].

13 February 1855 - A new manner of fitting the **firing-cap pouch** was confirmed (see Grenadier regiments) [57].

XLVI. LIFE-GUARDS HORSE-PIONEER SQUADRON. [*Leib-Gvardii Konno-Pionernyi eskadron.*]

11 February 1826 - Clerks and in general all non-combatant lower ranks were to have grey **riding-trousers** with wide red stripes [58]

15 September 1826 - Lower ranks who had completed the regulation number of years of faultless service but voluntarily remained on active duty were to wear **gold galloon** sewn onto the left sleeve, as described above in detail for Grenadier regiments [59].

1 January 1827 - Officers' **epaulettes** were to have small forged and stamped stars as rank distinctions, as described above [60].

31 July 1827 - Numbers and letters on the **covers** for shakos were ordered to be painted in yellow oil paint [61].

8 October 1827 - A new pattern of **saber** for lower combatant ranks was approved, straighter than before and with a brass hilt, black grip, and iron scabbard (Illus. 805) [62].

13 October 1827 – Instead of shoulder straps, combatant lower ranks were given **scaled epaulettes** for the coat, in the same color as the buttons, with a backing and strap of red cloth (Illus. 805). The fields of officers' epaulettes were also to be scaled [63].

14 December 1827 - The lower ranks' **chevrons** on the left sleeve established on 15 September were to be silver and made from non-commissioned officers' galloon [64].

24 March 1828 - It was forbidden for the **coats** of lower ranks to have cinches [*peretyazhki*] [65].

9 February 1828 - A new model of **shako** was issued, identical to that established at this time for the 1st Horse-Pioneer Squadron, but with the previous Guards badge [66].

24 April 1828 – There were changes in the uniforms of **non-combatant non-commissioned officers** and **craftsmen**, in all respects in agreement with the descriptions for the L.-Gds. Sapper Battalion above [67].

21 April 1829 – To replace the squadron's previous **shako plates**, new ones were prescribed, identical to those established on 24 April 1828 for the L.-Gds. Sapper Battalion (Illus. 806) [68].

9 July 1829 – The wide stripes on officers' and lower ranks' riding trousers were removed, leaving only piping on the side seams [69].

16 December 1829 – The black cuffs of officers' **frock coats** were changed to dark green, with red piping as before [70].

26 December 1829 - All squadron personnel were to have uniform **buttons** with a raised representation of the two-headed eagle prescribed for the shako plate [71].

26 September 1830 – White lining was prescribed for officers' **frock coats** [72].

13 April 1834 - **Pouches** and **pouch-belts** were to be of a new pattern with a smaller cover and narrower belt [73].

2 May 1834 - For better handling, the hilts of the **sabers** were ordered to be reworked in a new style as explained above in detail (see uniforms for Army Dragoon regiments) [74].

2 July 1834 – Lower ranks' previous leather **sword knots** with woolen tassels were replaced by ones made completely of leather [75].

7 December 1834 - When shakos were worn, the **shako lines** were prescribed not to reach to the waist, as before, but only halfway down the back [76].

15 January 1835 – All combatant non-commissioned officers in the squadron were prescribed one **pistol** each, to be carried with them in a special holster [77].

13 April 1835 – Rules were confirmed regarding the wear of officers' **shako lines** when in formation and out of it, in all respects identical to the descriptions above for Guards Horse Artillery [78].

31 January 1836 - Lower ranks' **greatcoats** were to have eleven buttons instead of twelve: six down the front, two on the collar tabs, two on the shoulder straps, and one behind on the flaps [79].

27 April 1836 - **Lower pompons** [*repeiki*] were to be lined with black leather [80].

9 October 1836 - In order to carry their **pistols**, trumpeters were to have holsters [*chushki*] attached to the saddle on the left side over the saddle cloth. For the cartridges they were to have pouches [*lyadunki*] with belts, like those of other lower ranks [81].

17 January 1837 – Rules were confirmed regarding wearing officers' sabers with the **frock coat**, as set forth in detail above for Guards Lancer regiments [82].

14 February 1837 - Trumpeters, who were prescribed pistols when in mounted formation and likewise pouches with belts for their cartridges, were ordered to also wear these **cartridge-pouches** when in dismounted formation [83].

15 July 1837 - A new pattern of officers' **sash** was approved, identical with that introduced at this time for the preceding troops and described above in detail (see Grenadier regiments) [84].

17 December 1837 – To introduce uniformity in officers' **epaulettes**, a new pattern was approved, i.e. with the addition of a fourth twist of thin braid [85].

11 January 1838 – A description of the officers' **saddle** prescribed for use on 6 March 1834 was confirmed, in all aspects in agreement with that set forth above (see Army Dragoon regiments) [86].

23 February 1838 - Regulations concerning the **pistol holsters** [*pistoletnyya chushki*] mandated for the saddle on 9 October 1836 were confirmed as laid out above for Army Dragoon regiments [87].

4 January 1839 - Officers' **riding-trousers** [*reituzy*] were not to have any bows or bands in front but rather worn completely plain in the manner prescribed for lower ranks [88].

16 October 1840 - A regulation concerning **silver chevrons** for lower ranks was confirmed as laid out above (see Guards Lancer regiments) [89].

23 January 1841 - The capes of officers' **greatcoats** were to be 1 arshin [28 inches] long as measured from the lower edge of the collar [90].

13 November 1841 - All combatant ranks were given a new pattern of **saber** identical with that introduced at this time for the L.-Gds. Horse-Grenadier and Dragoon regiments (Illus. 807) [91].

8 April 1843 - A new model **shako** was approved, lower than before and curving inward at the bottom, being identical to that confirmed at this time for the preceding troops. For distinguished different lower **ranks**, sewn-on trim [*nashivki*] was established for the shoulder straps of dress coats and greatcoats, based on the scheme prescribed for the 1st Horse-Pioneer Squadron, but with Army galloon replaced by Guards tape [92].

10 May 1843 - Cover flaps [*kryshki*] for **cartridge pouches** were to be (with the cover sewn to the box): 4-1/2 vershoks [8 inches] long, 4-7/8 vershoks [9 inches] wide at the top edge, and 5-5/8 vershoks [10 inches] wide along the bottom edge [93].

2 January 1844 - Officers were to have a **cockade** on the cap band of the forage cap, identical with that established for the preceding troops and described above (see Grenadier regiments) [94].

9 May 1844 – Shakos were replaced by **helmets** with **plumes**, of the same pattern and in accordance with the same regulations as in effect at this time for the L.-Gds. Sapper Battalion, but with the addition of a metallic edge to the front visor of the same color as the helmet's fittings (Illus. 808) [95].

21 September 1844 – The **non-commissioned officer standard-bearer** [*shtandartnyi unter-ofitser*], when in formation, was ordered to always have the cartridge pouch under the standard belt [96].

4 January 1845 - Officers' **helmets** were to have, on the right side under the chin-scales, a cockade, as described above (Illus. 809) [97].

9 August 1845 - In camp dress [*lagernaya forma*], **helmets** were ordered to be worn without plumes, even if personnel prescribed them were wearing their coats [*mundiry*] [98].

31 March 1846 - New-model **artillery sabers** and **dragoon muskets** were introduced, the manner and fitting of which was to be the same as for dragoons (Illus. 810) [99].

7 August 1846 - Approval was given to a description of fitting **firing-cap pouches** and packing **tin cases**, the **small valise**, and **percussion-cap turnscrew** (see Guards Dragoon regiments) [100].

13 September 1846 - New **holsters** [*kobury*] for officers' percussion pistols were confirmed (see Army Cuirassier reg) [101].

19 May 1847 – Noncombatant lower ranks were given gray **forage caps** (see Guards Infantry regiments) [102].

5 November 1847 – Lower ranks in mounted order were directed to wear, when circumstances required, **greatcoats** over the accouterments and using the sleeves, with the front open [103].

9 January 1848 - On those days when they were obliged to remain in ceremonial dress after the mounting of the guard, field and company-grade officers were permitted for walking-out to wear the **frock coat** and *chakchiry* pants with **helmet** and **plume** [104].

19 January 1848 – Confirmation was given to a description of the **firing-cap pouch** [*kapsulnaya sumochka*] with the cartridge-pouch (see Army Cuirassier regiments) [105].

25 April 1848 - All flaps and buttons were removed from **valises** [106].

9 and 25 November 1849 – A description of fitting the **helmet** was approved (see Grenadier regiments) [107].

24 December 1849 - The grip of the hilt of the **gold half-saber** awarded for bravery was to be gold [108].

5 March 1850 - The **bandolier** [*pantaler*] for the standard was to be 2-1/2 vershoks [4 3/8 inches] wide and 2 arshins [56 inches] long, lined with red velvet and silver trim on the outside, and with dark-green cloth on the inside [109].

30 March 1851 - Cartridge-pouch belts were to be 1 vershok [1-3/4 inches] wide, with the previous firing-cap pouch [110].

15 April 1851 - Approval was given to instructions for fitting straps to the **valise** for lower ranks in dismounted order (see Army Cuirassier regiments) [111].

3 January 1852 – Cases for the **firing nipples** [*sterzhni*] of percussion weapons, as introduced for Army Infantry on 8 July 1851, were confirmed for the L.-Gds. Horse-Pioneer Squadron [112].

26 January 1852 – The band on noncombatants' gray **forage caps** was prescribed to be the same color as combant lower ranks' collars [113].

13 August 1853 - Officers in the campaign dress of **frock coat** without sash were to wear the sword-belt over the coat [114].

15 November 1853 – Confirmation was given to a description of how to roll soldiers' **greatcoats** on the saddle, and of light-cavalry officers' **horse furniture** (see Army Cuirassier regiments) [115].

29 April 1854 - Campaign **greatcoats** were confirmed for officers (see Grenadier regiments) [116].

XLVII. GUARDS ENGINEERS. [*Gvardeiskie inzhenery.*]

11 February 1826 – Instead of their previous dark-green pants with high boots and gray riding-trousers with wide stripes, Guards Engineer officers were given long dark-green **pants** with red piping on the side seams and boots with the spurs driven in (Illus. 811) [117].

26 July 1826 – In **summer time**, when troop unit officers were in summer pants and gaiters, these Engineer officers were ordered to also wear summer pants of the pattern established on 11 February for dark-green pants (Illus. 812) [118].

18 August 1826– Guards Engineer officers, when on inspections of works outside the capital cities, were ordered to be in **half-uniform**, i.e. in frock coats with epaulettes, without swords, and wearing the forage cap [119].

1 January 1827 - Guards Engineer officers' **epaulettes** were to have small forged and stamped gold stars as rank distinctions, and of the same pattern and scheme for the preceding Guards troops [120].

16 December 1829 – The black cuffs on Guards Engineer officers' **frock coats** were changed to dark green, with red piping as before [121].

26 December 1829 – For Guards Engineer officers the **buttons** on dress coats, frock coats, and greatcoats were prescribed to have a raised image of a two-headed eagle and beneath it two crossed axes, identical to the buttons established at this time for the L.-Gds. Sapper Battalion and L.-Gds. Horse-Pioneer Squadron [122].

8 June 1832 – These officers were permitted to wear **moustaches** [123].

15 July 1837 - A new pattern of officers' **sash** was approved, identical to that described above (see Grenadier regiments) [124].

17 December 1837 - A new pattern of officers' **epaulette** was approved, identical with that introduced for the preceding troops, i.e. with the addition of a fourth twist of thin braid [125].

4 January 1839 – Guards Engineer officers' **pants** were ordered not to have any bows or bands on the front, but were to have them completely smooth in the manner established for army lower ranks [126].

23 January 1841 - The capes of officers' **greatcoats** were to be 1 arshin [28 inches] long as measured from the lower edge of the collar [127].

2 January 1844 – Guards Engineer officers were to have an elongated metallic **cockade** on the forage-cap band, identical to that introduced at this time for the preceding troops [128].

2 February 1846 – Instead of the hat, Guards Engineer officers were given **helmets**, as introduced in the L.-Gds. Sapper Battalion but with white plumes. Generals had the same helmets with a Guards infantry plate (Illus. 813)[129].

13 October 1849 – Instead of the épée [*shpaga*], infantry **half-sabers** [*polusabli*] were prescribed [130].

24 December 1849 - The grip on the hilt of the **gold half-saber** awarded for bravery was to be gold [131].

XLVIII. GUARDS GENERAL STAFF. [*Gvardeiskii General'nyi Shtab*.]

11 February 1826 – The previous pants with high boots and riding-trousers with wide stripes of Guards General Staff officers were replaced by long dark-green **pants** with red piping on the side seams and (Illus. 814) [132].

26 July 1826 – For **summer time**, when troop unit officers were in summer pants and gaiters, Guards General Staff officers were authorized summer pants identical to the dark-green ones established on 11 February (Illus. 815) [133].

18 August 1826 – When on survey duties outside the capital cities of St. Petersburg and Moscow, these officers were ordered to be in **half uniform** [*poluforma*], i.e. in frock coats with epaulettes, without sword, wearing the forage cap [134].

26 December 1829 – The uniform **buttons** of Guards General Staff officers were prescribed to have a raised image of a two-headed eagle [135].

In February 1831 – When on campaign, officers of the Guards General Staff were allowed to carry **half-sabers** [*polusabli*] as introduced on 12 December 1826 for Guards infantry officers and on 20 August 1830 for Army infantry officers, described above in detail (see Grenadier regiments) [136].

7 December 1844 – When not on duty, generals in the uniform of the Guards General Staff were prescribed white **plumes** for the hat instead of black. When on duty they were to wear the **helmets** introduced in the Guards infantry on 9 May 1844, except with silver fittings and a white plume (Illus. 816). The same helmets were prescribed for field and company-grade officers, and hats were discontinued (Illus. 816) [137].

4 January 1845 – A **cockade** was established for the helmet, on the right side under the scales, as described above (see Guards infantry and cavalry regiments) (Illus. 817) [138].

In addition to the changed noted here, the following orders for Guards Engineers were extended to the Guards General Staff with equal force: **8 June 1832** – on wearing moustaches; **15 July 1837** – on gold stars on epaulettes; **17 December 1837** – on the change in the pattern for officers' epaulettes; **4 January 1830** – on officers' pants and trousers; **23 January 1841** – on the new length for the cape on officers' greatcoats; **2 January 1844** – on the introduction of a cockade for the band on officers' forage caps.

14 September 1849 – A pattern for **percussion pistols** was confirmed (see Grenadier regiments) [139].

13 October 1849 – Instead of the épée [*shpaga*], infantry **half-sabers**[*polusabli*] were prescribed (Illus. 818) [140].

24 December 1849 - The grip on the hilt of the **gold half-saber** awarded for bravery was to be gold [141].

18 February 1854 – A **valise** and **greatcoat** to be carried on the saddle were established [142].

29 April 1854 – Campaign **greatcoats** were established for wartime, of the pattern confirmed for Army and Guards troops, with a black velvet collar and shoulder straps, piped red [143].

XLIX. LIFE-GUARDS GARRISON BATTALION. [*Leib-Gvardii Garnizonnyi batalion.*]

11 February 1826 - Officers and lower combatant ranks of the L.-Gds. Garrison Battalion were given **single-breasted coats** instead of double-breasted, with nine flat buttons in front, dark-green cuff flaps, and red piping down the front opening, from the bottom front to the skirts, and on the cuff flaps, and for officers—also on the pocket folds.

The former officers' grey riding-trousers and white pants with high boots and the lower ranks' same pants with knee gaiters were replaced with long dark-green **pants** of the pattern introduced for Guards infantry, with red piping on the side seams. Lower ranks at all times, and company-grade officers only in formation, were to wear black cloth **half-gaiters** fastened with five or six small metal buttons of the same color as the coat buttons (Illus. 819 and 820). When in such pants, a general, field-grade officer, and adjutant, as well as company-grade officers with troops, were ordered not to wear gaiters but have **boots** with spurs driven in. Along with these changes, the horizontal **belt for the knapsack** was to be between the two lower buttons on the front of the coat, while the **greatcoat** was to be carried on the knapsack rolled into a tube in its special oilskin case made of raven's-duck. Clerks and all noncombatant lower ranks in general were ordered to wear gray riding trousers without stripes [144].

10 May 1826 - Generals, field-grade officers, and those company-grade officers who were by regulation mounted when in formation, were ordered during the summer to wear white linen **pants** without integral spats [*kozyrki*], of the same pattern as previously described for the dark-green ones (Illus. 821). In addition, suede [*zamshevyya*] pants of the same pattern were permitted to be worn instead of the linen pants [145].

15 September 1826 - Lower ranks who had completed the regulation number of years of faultless service and had the right to be discharged but who voluntarily remained on active duty were to wear a **gold galloon** stripe sewn onto the left sleeve in addition to the yellow tape established on 29 March 1825 [146].

12 December 1826 – Officers' épées [*shpagi*] were replaced by **half-sabers** [*polusabli*] of the same pattern as introduced on 20 August 1830 for Army infantry and described above as part of the uniform and accouterments for Grenadier regiments (Illus. 821) [147].

1 January 1827 - Officers' **epaulettes** were to have small forged and stamped gold stars as rank distinctions, and of the same pattern and scheme as set forth above (see Guards heavey infantry regiments) [148].

31 July 1827 - Numbers and letters on the **covers** for shakos and pouches were ordered changed from yellow cloth to yellow oil paint [149].

14 December 1827 – The sewn-on **chevrons** established for lower ranks' left sleeves on 15 September 1826 were ordered to be of silver non-commissioned officers' galloon [150].

24 March 1828 - The **coats** of lower ranks were forbidden to have cinches [151].

24 April 1828 – All combatant ranks in the battalion were given new-pattern **shakos**, identical to those introduced for the preceding Guards infantry regiments, i.e. higher than before, without leather straps sewn onto the sides, with white cord around the top and small tassels with bows hanging from the right side level with the shako's lower edge. The **shako plate**, in connection with the shako's greater size, was also prescribed to be of a new pattern, somewhat altered and enlarged, of white tin as previously. Plumes, pompons, and chinscales remained unchanged (Illus. 822). Along with this the following changes were also introduced:

1. The width of the **crossbelt** and **swordbelt** was stipulated as 2 vershoks [3-1/2 inches], of the **knapsack shoulder belts**—1-1/2 vershoks [2-5/8 inches], and of the **belt across the chest** [*nagrudnyi remen*]—1-1/8 vershoks [2 inches].

2. **Knapsacks** [*rantsy*] were to be of calfskin as before but with black leather trim. The knapsack was prescribed to be 9 vershoks [15-3/4 inches] wide, 8 vershoks [14 inches] high, and 2-1/2 [4-3/8 inches] in depth. The length of the cover from the upper edge was 6 vershoks [10-1/2 inches].

3. All **noncombatant** lower ranks were given new pattern uniforms, identical to those established at this time for preceding Guards heavy and light infantry regiments and described above in detail [152].

18 May 1829 - Non-commissioned officers who had been recommended by higher command for promotion to officer rank by virtue of years of service were permitted to have **silver sword-knots** [153].

26 December 1829 – For all ranks uniform **buttons** were prescribed to have a raised image of the two-headed eagle as found on the shako plate [154].

8 June 1832 – Officers were permitted to wear **moustaches** [155].

3 January 1833 - **Cloth half-gaiters** were abolished for company-grade officers and lower ranks (Illus. 823). **Swordknots** were ordered retained only for those non-commissioned officers who had them in silver [156].

20 February 1833 - All combatant ranks were given new pattern **summer pants or trousers** [letniya pantalony ili bryuki], without buttons or integral spats (Illus. 824) [157].

16 April 1833 – Field and company-grade officers who had to be mounted when in formation were permitted to have **horses** with long tails [158].

26 September 1834 - Lower ranks were directed to wear the **knapsack** on two belts lying crosswise over the chest (Illus. 825)[159].

20 August 1835 – Officers were ordered to wear **knapsacks** only using two lacquered shoulder straps, without any cross strap over the chest. For lower ranks a linen case or pocket [kholshchevyi chekhol ili karman] for the forage cap was to be put on the outside of knapsack on the side that lay on the soldier's back. These cases were to be made from the linings of worn-out coats. For drummers the knapsack was to have one belt as before, worn over the left shoulder [160].

31 January 1836 - The lower ranks' **greatcoat** was to have nine buttons instead of ten: six along the front opening, two on the shoulder straps, and one on the flaps behind [161].

27 April 1836 - **Lower pompons** [repeiki] were ordered to be lined with black leather [162].

13 May 1836 – It was established that girths for officers' **saddles** were to be dark green with red stripes [163].

21 October 1836 - Shako **plumes** [sultany] were established to be 11 vershoks [19-1/4 inches] high from the triangular hair socket [tresovka] to the top, with an upper circumference of 5-2/3 vershoks [10 inches] and a lower one of 4 [7]. Their weight was not to be more than 54 zolotniks [8-1/10 ounces] [164].

14 January 1837 – The wooden parts of **entrenching tool** [shantsovyi instrument] handles were to be lacquered instead of painted with oil paints. The directives for the fitting and carrying of these tools were confirmed as laid out in detail above (see Grenadier regiments) [165].

15 July 1837 - A new pattern of officers' **sash** was approved, identical to that introduced for the preceding troops and described above (see Grenadier regiments) [166].

17 December 1837 – To achieve uniformity, a new pattern of officers' **epaulette** was approved, i.e. with the addition of a fourth twist of thin braid [167].

4 January 1839 - Officers' **pants** were ordered not to have any bows or bands on the front, but were to have them completely smooth in the manner established for lower ranks [168].

16 March 1839 - Lower ranks' **swordbelts** were to be 1-1/2 vershoks [2-3/5 inches] wide, while **drummers' crossbelts** were 2-1/2 vershoks [4-2/5 inches] wide, as before [169].

16 October 1840 – Rules regarding silver **chevrons** for lower ranks were confirmed, as set forth above for Guards Lancer regiments[170].

23 January 1841 - The capes of officers' **greatcoats** were to be 1 arshin [28 inches] long as measured from the lower edge of the collar [171].

8 April 1843 – All combatant ranks were given new model **shakos**, 4-3/4 vershoks [8-3/8 inches] high and curving slightly inward toward the bottom. New dimensions were prescribed for shako plumes: 9-3/4 vershoks [17 inches] high from the hair socket to the top, with an upper circumference of 5-1/4 vershoks [9-3/16 inches] and a lower one of 3-1/2 [6-1/8]. **Rank distinctions** for lower ranks were established in the form of trim sewn onto the shoulder straps of coats and greatcoats following the scheme prescribed for the preceding Guards heavy and light infantry. On this same date it was directed that **drum-majors' epaulettes** [tambur-mazhorskie epolety] have red silk between the braided gold thread and in the hanging fringe so as to be more easily distinguished from epaulettes for generals. [172].

10 May 1843 – Cover flaps [kryshki] for **cartridge pouches** were to be, without any sharp break with the cover sewn to the box, 5 vershoks [8-3/4 inches] high: 5-1/2 vershoks [9-5/8 inches] wide at the top edge, and 6 vershoks [10-1/2 inches] wide along the bottom edge [173].

2 January 1844 - Officers were to have an elongated metallic **cockade** on the forage-cap band, identical to that introduced for preceding troops and described above (see Grenadier regiments) [174].

9 May 1844 - Shakos were replaced by **helmets** [kaski] of black lacquered leather with two cockades, metal fittings the same color as the buttons, a horse-hair plume (red for musicians and black for other ranks), and the previous plate, following the pattern of helmets introduced at this time for preceding troops (Illus. 826) [175].

20 May 1844 – With approval given to a new scheme for differentiating the **forage caps** of lower ranks, they remained dark green as before, with piping around the upper crown and on both edges of the band prescribed to be red, while the band itself was also dark green with a cut-out company number and the Cyrillic letter R backed by yellow cloth. Officers had the same forage caps but without numbers or letters and with a visor [176].

17 November 1844 – Confirmation was given to a description of how to keep and preserve helmet plumes, as set fort in detail above (see Grenadier regiments) [177].

4 January 1845 - Officers' **helmets** were to have a cockade on the right side under the chin-scales, identical to that introduced at this time for the preceding troops and described above in detail for Grenadier regiments [178]. Apart from these changes, the following orders presented above for the uniforms and equipment of Guards infantry were extended with equal force to all ranks of the Guards Garrison Battalion: **23 June 1846** – on fitting firing-cap pouches; **19 April 1849** – on English signal bugles; **9 November 1849** – on fitting helmets; **24 December 1849** – on gold half-sabers awarded for courage; **17 January 1851** – on rules for taking up and turning back greatcoat skirts; **29 April 1854** – on campaign greatcoats for officers.

L. GUARDS INVALID COMPANIES. [*Gvardeiskiya invalidnyya roty.*]

11 February 1826 - Officers and lower combatant ranks of Guards Invalid companies were given **single-breasted coats** instead of double-breasted, with nine flat buttons in front, dark-green cuff flaps, and red lining on the tails. The existing officers' pants with high boots and the lower ranks' pants with knee gaiters were replaced with long dark-green **pants** of the pattern introduced at this time in the L.-Gds. Garrison Battalion, but without piping on the side seams. Lower ranks at all times, and company-grade officers only in formation, were to wear black cloth **half-gaiters** under these pants, fastened with five or six small metal buttons of the same color as the coat buttons (Illus. 827). Along with this change, the horizontal **belt for the knapsack** was to be between the two lower buttons on the front of the coat, while the **greatcoat** was to be carried on the knapsack rolled into a tube in its special oilskin case made of raven's-duck [179].

12 December 1826 – Officers' épées [*shpagi*] were replaced by half-sabers [*polusabli*] of the same pattern as introduced in the Guards Infantry [180].

24 April 1828 – Officers and lower ranks of Guards Invalid companies were given new-pattern helmets and helmet plates identical to those introduced for the L.-Gds. Garrison Battalion, without plumes, as before (Illus. 828) [181].

5 June 1832 - Guards Invalid Company No. 16, newly formed to support the St.-Petersburg police, had the same uniform clothing and weapons as other Guards Invalid companies, but was ordered to not have knapsacks, and to wear the short sword [*tesak*] on a black lacquered sword belt instead of a white one (Illus. 829) [182].

3 January 1833 - **Cloth half-gaiters** were abolished for company-grade officers and lower ranks, as were shako covers and swordknots for non-commissioned officers and privates (Illus. 830). **Swordknots** were ordered retained only for those non-commissioned officers who had received them in silver [183].

20 February 1833 – Officers and lower ranks were given new pattern **summer pants or trousers** [*letniya pantalony ili bryuki*] without buttons or integral spats (Illus. 831) [184].

8 April 1843 – Officers of Guards Invalid companies were prescribed **sashes** along with officers of mobile invalid companies and invalid commands (Illus. 832). On this same date new-pattern **shakos** were confirmed for all ranks, lower than before and and slightly curved inward at the bottom, identical to those introduced for preceding troops (Illus. 832). Sewn-on tape for the **shoulder straps** of sergeants, non-commissioned officers, and corporals were established in accordance with the scheme described above for Guards heavy infantry regiments [185].

9 May 1844 – For officers and lower ranks shakos were replaced by **helmets** with black plumes, identical to those introduced at this time in the L.-Gds. Garrison Battalion (Illus. 833) [186].

4 January 1845 - Officers' **helmets** were to have a cockade on the right side under the chin-scales, identical to that introduced for the preceding troops (Illus. 834) [187].

Apart from the changes described here, the following orders presented above (see uniforms and weapons for the L.-Gds. Garrison Battalion) were extended with equal force to all ranks of Guards Invalid companies: **15 September 1826** – on sewn-on gold stripes for lower ranks; **1 January 1827** – on small gold stars for officers' epaulettes; **1 July 1827** – on the numbers and letters on lower ranks' shako covers to be painted instead of cloth; **14 December 1827** – on sewn-on silver stripes for lower ranks; **24 March 1828** – on cinches being forbidden on lower ranks' uniforms; **24 April 1828** – on narrowing the width of the sword belt and on changes in the knapsack; **18 May 1829** – on silver sword knots for non-commissioned officers; **26 December 1829** – on the introduction for all ranks of buttons with the coat-of-arms instead of being flat; **8 July 1832** – on officers wearing moustaches; **20 January 1833** – on keeping shako covers; **26 September 1834** – on introducing cross straps for knapsacks; **20 August 1835** – on knapsacks for officers and lower ranks; **31 January 1836** – on reducing the number of buttons on lower ranks' greatcoats; **27 April 1836** – on shako pompons; **17 December 1837** – on changing the pattern for epaulettes; **4 January 1839** – on officers' pants; **16 March 1839** – on the narrowing of lower ranks' sword belts; **16 October 1844** – on sewn-on chevrons for lower ranks; **23 January 1841** – on officers' greatcoats; **2 January 1844** – on the introduction of cockades for officers' forage caps; **17 November 1844** – on helmet plumes for lower ranks; **9 November 1849** – on fitting the helmet; **24 December 1849** – gold half-sabers awarded for courages; **17 January 1851** – on rules for taking up and turning back the skirts of soldiers' greatcoats.

LI. GUARDS ÉQUIPAGE, its ARTILLERY COMMAND, and the GUARDS BARGE COMPANY.
[*Gvardeiskii ekipazh, v artilleriiskoi egokomande i v gvardeiskoi lastovoi rote.*]

11 February 1826 – Lower ranks of the Guards Équipage, its Artillery Command, and the Guards Barge Company, were given a single-breasted **jacket** [*kurtka*] in place of double-breasted, with nine flat buttons in front. The parade **coats** of officers of the Guards Équipage and its Artillery Command were also prescribed to be single-breasted with nine buttons just as for lower ranks (Illus. 835 and 836), while their undress coats [*vitsemundiry*] were left as before. Along with this the **knapsack's** horizontal cross strap, following the example of Army troops, was prescribed to be worn between two lower buttons on the coat's front opening, while the **greatcoat** was to carried on the knapsack rolled into a tube and kept in a special oilskin case made from raven's duck [188].

15 September 1826 - Lower ranks who had completed the regulation number of years of faultless service and received the right to discharge yet voluntarily remained on active duty were to wear, above the yellow tape chevrons on the left sleeve established on 29 March 1825, an additional gold galloon **chevron** [189].

1 January 1827 – For officers of the Guards Équipage's Artillery Command, in order to distinguish **rank**, there were established small silver stamped stars for the epaulettes, of the same appearance and to be worn according to the same scheme as set forth above for Guards heavy infantry regiments [190].

1 July 1827 – **Skippers** [*Shkipera*] in the Guards Équipage's Barge Company were retitled with corresponding military officers' ranks and prescribed the same uniform clothing and arms as this équipage's officers, but with silver instead of gold (Illus. 837) [191].

31 July 1827 – Numbers and letters on **shako** and **pouch** covers, instead of being in yellow cloth, were ordered to be painted in yellow oilpaints [192].

14 December 1827 – The sewn-on **galloon** established for lower ranks' left sleeves in the Guards Barge Company on 15 September 1826 was ordered to be silver, following the color and pattern of non-commissioned officers' galloon [193].

24 March 1828- The **jackets** of lower ranks were forbidden to have cinches [194].

24 April 1828 – Red piping was established for the **jackets** and greatcoats of lower ranks in the Guards Équipage's Artillery Company, instead of white, and this piping was added to the lower edge of the collar. Officers, following the example of lower ranks, were prescribed red piping on the dress coat, undress coat, frock coat, and greatcoat (Illus. 838) [195].

On this same day there were the following changes in regard to uniform clothing and accouterments:

1. A new-pattern **shako** was given, higher than before, without leather straps as trimming on the sides, identical to that introduced at this time for preceding troops. There was also a new pattern for decorative cords, these being a cord around the top of the shako, cords hanging down the right side level with the shako's lower edge, small tassels, and bows. In the Guards Équipage and Guards Barge Company the shako cords of lower ranks were left white, as before, while in the Artillery Command they were red. For non-commissioned officers the tassels with bows also remained in the previous colors: white, black, and orange, while officers' cords were all silver. The shako plate, chinscales, and pompons for all ranks remained without any changes (Illus. 838 and 839).

2. Round **pompons** were added to these shakos, being the same colors as the previous turnip-shaped pompons: dark green in the Guards Équipage and Guards Barge Company, and red in the Artillery Command, but silver for officers (Il. 838 and 839).

3. The **pouch belt** and **sword-belt** were prescribed to be 2 vershoks [3-1/2 inches] wide; the **shoulder belts for the knapsack**—1-1/2 vershok [2-5/8 inches]; and the **belt across the chest**—1-1/8 vershok [2 inches].

4. All noncombatant lower ranks were given dark-green single-breasted **frock coats** with the same cuffs, collar, and shoulder straps as for combatants, while pants were to be gray without any piping on the side seams (Illus. 840) [196].

16 January 1830 – All ranks in the équipage were prescribed uniform **buttons** with the raised image of a two-headed eagle, behind the middle of which were two crossed anchors. The Artillery Command was given the same buttons but with the addition of two crossed cannons under the eagle's talons [197].

14 June 1830 – The Guards Barge Company was prescribed uniform **buttons** with the same coat-of-arms as established for the Guards Équipage on 16 January, but white, as before [198].

15 October 1830 – For all équipage ranks the piping on both edges of the **forage cap's** band was established to be white instead of the previous red [199].

2 November 1830 – All combatant ranks of the Guards Équipage, its Artillery Command, and the Guards Barge Company were given **shako plates** the same color as their buttons, of a new, somewhat altered and enlarged pattern (Illus. 841) [200].

21 November 1830 – In order to distinguish **officer rank** in the Guards Équipage, small stamped and forged silver stars were established for the epaulettes: 1 for midshipmen, 3 for lieutenants, 2 for captain-lieutenants, 3 for 2nd rank captains, and none for 1st rank captains [201].

12 December 1830 – **Officer candidates** [*yunkery*] in the Guards Équipage were prescribed the same uniform clothing as this équipage's combatant non-commissioned officers [202].

8 June 1832 – Officers were allowed to wear **moustaches** [203].

3 January 1833 – **Shako covers** were withdraws from officers, and from lower combatant ranks—shako covers, cartridge pouch covers, and sword knots [204].

20 January 1833 – **Shako covers** were left as before [205].

26 September 1834 – Lower ranks were ordered to wear **knapsacks** on two straps crossing over the chest (Illus. 842) [206].

20 August 1835 – Officers were directed to wear the **knapsack** using only two lacquered shoulder belts, without any straps over the front of the body or chest (Illus. 843). For lower ranks a linen case or pocket for the forage cap was to be put on the outside of the knapsack on the side that lay on the soldier's back. For drummers the knapsack was worn over the shoulder on one belt as before, worn over the left shoulder [207].

31 January 1836 - The lower ranks' **greatcoat** was to have nine buttons instead of ten: six down the front, two on the shoulder straps, and one on the flaps behind [208].

27 April 1836 - **Lower pompons** [*repeiki*] were to be lined with black leather [209].

13 May 1836 - Girths for officers' **saddles** in the Guards Équipage were to be dark green with red stripes [210].

17 December 1837 - Approval was given to a new pattern of officers' **epaulette** identical to that introduced at this time for the preceding troops and Guards infantry, i.e. with the addition of a fourth twist of thin braid [211].

4 January 1839 - Officers were not to have any bows or bands on the front of their **pants** or **trousers**. These were to be worn completely plain in the manner prescribed for lower ranks [212].

16 March 1839 - Lower ranks' **sword belts** and **crossbelts** were to be 1-1/2 vershoks [2-3/5 inches] wide, while drummers' **crossbelts** were 2-1/2 vershoks [4-2/5 inches] wide, as before [213].

16 October 1840 - A regulation was confirmed concerning sewn-on **gold and silver chevrons** for lower ranks, as laid out above for Guards Lancer regiments [214].

23 January 1841 - The capes of officers' **greatcoats** were to be 1 arshin [28 inches] long as measured from the lower edge of the collar [215].

8 April 1843 – On officers' **shabracks** in the Guards Équipage, white piping instead of red was prescribed along the edges of the gold galloon (Illus. 844). In order to be more easily distinguished from generals' epaulettes, it was directed that **drum-majors' epaulettes** have red silk interwoven in the braided gold threads and in hanging fringe (Illus. 845). On this same day a new pattern **shako** curving inward at the bottom was approved, identical to that confirmed at this time for the preceding troops. For distinguishing between the lower ranks, sewn-on tape was established for the **shoulder straps** of jackets and greatcoats, following the same scheme as set forth above for Guards heavy infantry regiments [216].

10 May 1843 - Cover flaps for **cartridge pouches**, sewn to the box, were to be: 5 vershoks [8-3/4 inches] long without a sharp bend, 5-1/2 vershoks [9-5/8 inches] wide at the top edge, and 6 vershoks [10-1/2 inches] wide along the bottom edge [217].

2 January 1844 - Officers were to have an elongated metal **cockade** on the band of the forage cap, identical with that introduced at this time for preceding Army and Guards troops (Illus. 846) [218].

5 May 1844 – A new scheme for the different **forage caps** for lower ranks was confirmed, based on which they were left dark green as before and with white piping around the top. In the Guards Équipage and Guards Barge Company the band was dark green with white piping along both edges, and cut out and backed by yellow cloth—the company number and Cyrillic letter R, and the letters L.R. in the Barge Company. In the Guards Équipage's Artillery Command the band was of black plissé with two red lines of piping, along both edges, and the Cyrillic letters A.R. cut out and backed by yellow cloth. For officers the forage cap was the same as for lower ranks but, as before, without numbers or letters and with a visor, and in the Artillery Command it also had the plissé band replaced by velvet [219].

9 September 1844 – **Shakos** of the standard navy pattern were confirmed for all combatant ranks of the Guards Équipage and its Artillery and Barge companies. This had horsehair plumes (red for musicians, black for other ranks); plates and chinscales remained as before (Illus. 847, 848, and 849) [220].

4 January 1845 - Officers' shakos were to have a **cockade** on the front, level with the shako's top edge, identical to that introduced for preceding Army and Guards troops and described above (see Grenadier regiments) (Illus. 850) [221].

9 January 1848 - On those days when they were obliged to remain in ceremonial dress after the mounting of the guard, officers were permitted for walking-out to wear the **frock coat** with **shako** and **plume** [222].

24 December 1849 - The grip of the hilt of the **gold half-saber** awarded for bravery was to be gold [223].

28 December 1852 – For generals, field and company-grade officers, and adjutants of the Guards Équipage, who were mounted when in formation, there were prescribed: for parade dress—**shabracks** of the previous pattern, and for campaign dress—newly introduced undress shabracks [*vitse-chepraki*] of the pattern established for Guards infantry regiments, but with white edging instead of red (Illus. 851) [224].

29 April 1854 – Campaign **greatcoats** were confirmed for officers, after the example of Guards regiments [225].

LII. INSTRUCTIONAL TROOPS. [*Uchebnyya voiska*.]
INSTRUCTIONAL CARABINIER REGIMENT [*Uchebnyi Karabinernyi polk*.]

11 February 1826 – Officers and lower ranks in the Instructional Carabinier Regiment were prescribed single-breasted instead of double-breasted **coats**, with flat buttons, as were introduced at this time for other Army infantry troops, with red piping along the front opening and from the opening to the skirttails, and with red cuff flaps. Along with this change, long dark-green pants were also introduced, with red piping and black cloth **half-gaiters** [*polushtiblety*] (for company-grade officers only when in formation and on parade) buttoned with five or six small brass buttons (Illus. 852 and 853). Generals, field-grade officers, and adjutants were prescribed boots with the **spurs** driven in.

Following the example of the rest of the infantry, in the Instructional Carabinier Regiment the horizontal belt for the **knapsack** was ordered to be worn between the two lower coat buttons, and the greatcoat was to be rolled into a tube inside a special oilskin case made of raven's-duck (Illus. 852) [226].

10 May 1826 - Generals, field-grade officers, and adjutants who had to be mounted when in formation, were during the summer ordered to wear white linen **pants** without integral spats [*kozyrki*], of the same pattern as the dark-green described above (Illus. 854). Instead of the linen pants, they were also allowed to wear suede pants of the same pattern [227].

22 October 1826 - In connection with the establishment of two carabinier regiments instead of one, titled the **1st** and **2nd Carabiniers**, the first was prescribed the number 1, and the second—2, to be on officers' epaulettes in silver and to be cut out on lower ranks' shoulder straps and backed by red cloth (Illus. 855) [228].

1 January 1827 – In order to distinguish **rank**, small forged or stamped silver stars were established for officers' epaulettes, of the same appearance and worn according to the same scheme as was prescribed at this time for all other Army infantry [229].

31 July 1827 - Numbers and letters on **shako** and **cartridge-pouch covers**, instead of being of yellow cloth, were ordered to be painted on with yellow oil paint [230].

24 March 1828 - The **coats** of lower ranks were forbidden to have cinches [231].

24 April 1828 – A new-pattern **shako** was introduced in both carabinier regiments, with pompons for jägers and marksmen that were the same as in Army carabinier regiments but without figures or numbers in the plate's grenade (Illus. 856 and 857). The **pouch belt** and **sword belt** were prescribed to be 2 vershoks [3-1/2 inches] wide; the **shoulder belts for the knapsack**—1-1/2 vershoks [2-5/8 inches]; and the **belt across the chest**—1-1/8 vershoks [2 inches]. **Knapsacks** were to have but with black leather trim all around (Illus. 856). The knapsack was to be 9 vershoks [15-3/4 inches] broad, 8 vershoks [14 inches] high, and 2-1/2 vershoks [4-3/8 inches] wide. The length of the cover (from the upper edge) was 6 vershoks [10-1/2] inches. All noncombatant non-commissioned officers were given dark-green single-breasted frock coats with the same cuffs, collar and shoulder straps as for combatants, along with gray pants with red piping (Illus. 857). Noncombatant craftsmen, as well as medical orderlies, had the same pants as noncombatants and were prescribed gray jackets of the same cut as dress coats (Illus. 857) [232].

18 May 1829 - Non-commissioned officers who had been recommended by higher command for promotion to officer rank by virtue of years of service were permitted to wear **silver sword knots** [233].

26 December 1829- All combatant ranks were prescribed uniform **buttons** with the raised image of a grenade, and on the grenade—a figure of the regimental number [234].

20 August 1830 – Officers' épées were replaced by **half-sabers** with black scabbards and gilded brass fittings [235].

8 June 1832 – Officers were allowed to wear **moustaches** [236].

3 January 1833 - Cloth **half-gaiters** [*polushtiblety*] were abolished for company-grade officers and lower ranks, and sword knots were to be kept only for those non-commissioned officers who had received them in silver [237].

28 January 1833 – The existing **cartridge-pouch badges** were ordered replaced by grenades with three flames, and in the center of the shield on the grenade there was to be a cutout figure depicting the regimental number (Illus. 858) [238].

20 February 1833 - All combatant ranks were given new pattern **summer pants** [*pantalony*], or **breeches** [*bryuki*], without buttons or integral spats [*kozyrki*] (Illus. 859) [239].

5 May 1833 – Numbers or figures on **shako plates** were prescribed to be affixed rather than cut out: of tin for lower ranks and silvered for officers (Illus. 860) [240].

25 February 1834 – The newly established **3rd Carabinier Regiment** was prescribed the same uniforms as the 1st and 2nd Carabinier Regiments with only the number being different [241].

26 September 1834 - Lower combatant ranks were ordered to wear the **knapsack** on two belts lying crosswise over the chest (Illus. 861) [242].

3 April 1835 – With the redesignation of the **3rd Carabinier Regiment** as the **4th** and the establishment of a new 3rd Carabinier Regiment, this last unit was left with, and the first unit prescribed, the same uniforms as for the 1st and 2nd Carabinier Regiments, with the only difference being the numbers on shako plates, buttons, epaulettes, and shoulder straps [243].

20 August 1835 – It was laid down that:

  1.) Officers were to wear the **knapsack** using only two lacquered shoulder belts without any horizontal strap over the chest.

  2.) For lower ranks a **linen case,** or pocket, for the forage cap was to be put on the outside of the knapsack on the side that lay on the soldier's back. These cases were to be made from the linings of wornout coats.

  3.) For drummers the **knapsack** was to have one belt as before, worn over the left shoulder [244].

31 January 1836 - Lower ranks' **greatcoats** were to have nine buttons instead of ten: six along the front opening, two on the shoulder straps, and one on the flap behind [245].

27 April 1836 – **Pompons** were ordered to be lined with black leather [246].

13 May 1836 - **Girths** for officers' saddles were to be dark green with red stripes [247].

21 October 1836 - **Shako plumes** in carabinier platoons were to be 11 vershoks [19-1/4 inches] high from the triangular socket to the top, with an upper circumference of 5-2/3 vershoks [10 inches] and a lower one of 4 vershoks [7 inches]. Its weight was to be not more than 54 zolotniks [8-1/10 ounces] [248].

14 January 1837 - Handles of **entrenching tools** were no longer to be painted with oil-based paint, but rather the wood was to be varnished, and directives for carrying and fitting these tools were confirmed, as described above in detail (see Grenadier regiments) [249].

15 July 1837 - Officers were given a new pattern of **sash** that instead of the previous wide lace had narrow silver lace with three stripes of light-orange and black silk, and was tied with its entire width between the two lower buttons of the coat [250].

17 December 1837 – **Regimental staff-hornists**, when they had to be mounted when in formation during summertime, were to have, instead of knapsacks, cavalry pattern valises. Their horses were to have bridles, and their saddles were to be of the model for mounted artillerymen, without a shabrack or saddlecloth [251].

4 January 1839 – Generals and field and company-grade officers were not to have any bows or bands on the front of their **pants** or **trousers**. These were to be worn completely smooth in the manner prescribed for lower ranks [252].

16 March 1839 - Lower ranks' **pouch belts** and **sword belts**, which were originally 2-1/8 vershoks [3-7/8 inches] wide and then, since 1828, 2 vershoks [3-1/2 inches] wide, were prescribed to be 1-1/2 vershoks [2-5/8 inches] wide. **Drummers' crossbelts** were to be as before, 2-1/2 vershoks [4-2/5 inches] wide [253].

23 January 1841 - The capes of officers' **greatcoats** were to be 1 arshin [28 inches] long as measured from the lower edge of the collar [254].

8 April 1843 – New-pattern **shakos** and **plumes** were confirmed, identical to those established at this time for Carabinier regiments (Illus. 862). Sewn-on tape was established for the **shoulder straps** of non-commissioned officers and corporals, described above in detail for Grenadier regiments. At this same time a new pattern of **drum major's epaulette** was confirmed, identical to that described above for Grenadier regiments [255].

10 May 1843 - The covers of **cartridge-pouches**, sewn onto the body of the pouch, were to measure, without any sharp bend or break on top, 5 vershoks [8-3/4 inches] long, 5-1/2 vershoks [9-5/8 inches] wide at the top edge, and 6 vershoks [10-1/2 inches] wide at the bottom edge [256].

2 January 1844 – Officers' forage caps were to have an oblong metal **cockade** on the front of the band, in the same colors as the cockade on officers' hats [257].

8 January 1844 - **Staff-hornists**, when mounted in formation, were permitted to have spurs [258].

9 May 1844 – Instead of shakos, all combatant ranks in instructional carabinier regiments were given **helmets** with plumes, of the same pattern as for Carabinier regiments in the Guards Corps, and with the previous plate (Illus. 863) [259].

4 January 1845 – Officers' **helmets** were to have, on the right side under the chin-scales, a metal **cockade** patterned after the one worn on hats [Illus. 864] [260].

9 August 1845 – When in camp dress the **helmet** was to be worn without the plume, even if those personnel entitled to plumes were wearing dress coats [261].

In addition, all the directives presented above for Carabinier regiments in the Guards Corps were extended with equal force to instructional carabinier regiments: **23 June 1816** – on fitting and wearing firing-cap pouches; **9 January 1848** – on the uniform for walking out on holidays; **19 April 1849** – on signal bugles; **14 September 1849** – on officers' percussion pistols; **17 January 1851** – on taking up greatcoat skirts; **8 July 1851** – on abolishing frizzen covers; **20 October 1851** – on items in the knapsack; **26 January 1852** – on noncombatant lower ranks' forage caps; **3 January 1853** – on noncombatant lower ranks' frock coats; **29 April 1854** – on officers' campaign greatcoats; **13 February 1855** – on on fitting firing-cap pouches.

INSTRUCTIONAL CAVALRY SQUADRON [*Uchebnyi Kavaleriiskii eskadron.*]

11 February 1826 – Clerks and in general all noncombatant lower ranks were prescribed gray **riding trousers** with wide red stripes [262].

10 June 1826 – The wide stripes were removed from the gray **riding trousers**, and only piping on the side seams was prescribed, the same color as the collar—i.e. red (Illus. 865) [263].

1 January 1827 - Small forged and stamped stars on officers' epaulettes were established to distinguish **rank**, of the same appearance and worn according to the same scheme as in the rest of the cavalry [264].

31 May 1827 – Round **pompons** were established for the shako: of yellow wool for lower ranks and silver for officers (Illus. 866) [265].

31 July 1827 – Numbers and letters on **shako covers** were ordered to be painted with yellow oil paint [266].

8 October 1827 – New-pattern **sabers** were established for lower ranks, with a brass hilt, black grip, and iron scabbard, and straighter than before (Illus. 866) [267].

13 October 1827 – Instead of woolen epaulettes with fringes, lower ranks' coats were to have **scaled epaulettes** of yellow brass, without fringes, the same color as the buttons, with a red cloth lining and trim and small cross straps of yellow woolen tape with a red stripe (Illus. 866). Along with this, the fields of officers' epaulettes were also prescribed to be scaled [268].

10 November 1827 - Officers and lower ranks were prescribed red **cuff flaps** with three buttons and dark-green piping. This piping was also to be on the collar, cuffs, and skirt turnbacks (Illus. 866) [269].

9 February 1828 – New-pattern **shakos** were given, 5-1/2 vershoks [9-5/8 inches] high with an upper diameter not less than 5-5/8 vershoks [9-7/8 inches] or more than 6 vershoks [10-1/2 inches], and the lower diameter to be the same according to the size of the head. The upper lacquered edge was to be 5/16 vershok [1/2 inch] wide, with a yellow pompon and cords, but silver for officers. The shako plate remained as before (Illus. 867) [270].

24 April 1828 – Instead of the grey coats previously used, all **non-combatant** non-commissioned officers were given dark-green **frock coats** with one row of buttons and the same collar, cuffs, and shoulder straps as for combatants. **Pants** were to be gray with red piping on the side seams. Instead of coats, non-combatant master-craftsmen lower ranks, as well as infirmary orderlies, were to wear jackets of gray cloth of the same pattern as the coat, while pants were to be as for the preceding non-combatants [271].

20 December 1828 – New-pattern **shako plates** were confirmed, of the model established for Army Dragoon regiments but with a cut-out Cyrillic letter U. instead of a number (Illus. 868) [272].

16 December 1829 – The cuffs on officers' **frock coats**, instead of being red, were prescribed to be the same color as the coat—dark green, with red piping [273].

26 December 1829 - All combatant ranks were prescribed uniform **buttons** with the raised image of a single-flame grenade [274].

23 January 1830 – It was ordered that **epaulettes** have a white metal Cyrillic letter U on them, and that for lower ranks the epaulettes not be trimmed with yellow tape [275].

24 September 1830 – The lining of officers' **frock coats** was directed to be the same color as the coat itself—dark green [276].

25 November 1830 – The dark-green *chakchiry* **pants** with wide stripes kept for parades was discontinued [277].

1 September 1832 – All combatant non-commissioned officers were given **muskets** [278].

16 March 1833 – **Undress coats** for field and company-grade officers were discontinued [279].

19 March 1833 – **Bandoleers** were withdrawn, and the hooks that had been on them were ordered to be on the pouch crossbelt [280].

5 May 1833 – The letters on **shako plates** were prescribed to affixed rather than cut out, of tin for lower ranks and silvered for officers (Illus. 869)[281].

24 December 1833 – Combatant lower ranks were given lancer pattern **girdles**: dark-green central part and piping, red edges (Illus. 869)[282].

6 April 1834 – **Muskets** were ordered carried over the shoulder on a strap rather than in a saddle bucket, in accordance with the newly confirmed method. The buckets on the saddle were therefore removed (Illus. 870)[283].

13 April 1834 – New-pattern **cartridge pouches** and **cross straps** were established, with a smaller pouch lid and and a narrower strap [284].

2 May 1834 - In order that **sabers** might be better handled, it was ordered that their hilts be reworked according to a new pattern, so that the straight arch, where it joins the headpiece, was sawn off even with the curved part, while the small flat part on the grip's brass trim, and this trim itself where it is pressed on by the thumb, were to be cut smooth[285].

30 June 1834 - On **muskets** the lower small handles for the sling, instead of being tightly fixed to an ear-shaped bracket set at the trigger guard, were directed to be made with screws. Moreover, special brackets with screws drilled into them were to be made for fixing the handles to the butt [286].

3 December 1834 – **Pistols** were withdrawn from the squadron [287].

7 December 1834 - **Shako cords**, when worn, were ordered to no longer reach to the waist, but only halfway down the back [288].

4 January 1835 – Grayish-blue [*sero-sinevatyi*] cloth **gloves** were introduced for privates. They were to be made from worn-out riding trousers and worn only when infantry troops are wearing their mittens [*rukavitsy*]. Non-commissioned officers kept their deerskin gloves as before [289].

20 February 1835 – In connection with pistols being withdrawn, the **ramrod** on the cartridge pouch was also withdrawn [290].

13 April 1835 - When in formation, officers were ordered to use a toggle to fasten one end of the **shako cord** to a loop made behind the shako using the cord itself, and at all other times, when officers were not in formation and had to take off the shako, this cord was to be detached from the loop, whereupon it was left around the neck with its slide, which was to be in back at the middle of the neck, and the end with the toggle was to be fastened to the second coat button from the top so that the cord passed under the right arm and over the pouch belt [291].

19 July 1835 – A description was confirmed of a leather **holster** in which to carry the pistol, and the manner of attaching it, as set forth in detail above for Dragoon regiments [292].

22 November 1835 - For greater convenience when riding, copper **kettles** were ordered to be strapped to the right side of the valises and not to the left [293].

31 January 1836 – Instead of ten buttons on lower ranks' **greatcoats**, nine were prescribed: six down the front, two on the shoulder straps, and one behind on the flaps [294].

27 April 1836 - **Pompons** were ordered to be backed with black leather [295].

5 May 1836 - New pattern **sword belts** were introduced, with slings and a strap with a small hook for the saber. The slings and strap were not movable, but sewn firmly to the sword belt [296].

9 October 1836 – For their **pistols**, trumpeters were prescribed carriers fastened to the saddle over the saddlecloth on the left side. For cartridges they were to have pouches with belts, as other lower ranks (Illus. 871) [297].

17 January 1837 - When wearing the **frock coat** without the sash, field and company-grade officers were ordered to wear the **saber** under the frock, attaching the upper ring to the hook next to the first sling and putting the hilt through an specially made pocket, in the same way as half-sabers and swords are worn in the Infantry. When wearing the frock coat with the sash, however, the saber was to be over the coat, left free on its slings and not hung onto the hook [298].

14 February 1837 - Trumpeters, who were prescribed **pistols** when in mounted formation and—for cartridges—pouches with belts, were ordered to also wear these when in dismounted formation [299].

15 July 1837 - A new pattern of officers' **sash** was confirmed, identical with that described above for Instructional Carabinier regiments [300].

17 December 1837 - In order to introduce uniformity in the style of officers' **epaulettes**, confirmation was given to a pattern with an additional, fourth, twist of narrow braid [301].

23 February 1838 – The regulations of 9 October 1836 concerning **pistol holders** on the saddle were confirmed, as laid out in detail above (see Army Dragoon regiments) [302].

4 January 1839 - The **riding trousers** of field and company-grade officers were ordered not to have any bows or bands in front but rather worn completely plain, in agreement with the style established for lower ranks [303].

23 January 1841 - The capes of officers' **greatcoats** were to be 1 arshin [28 inches] long as measured from the bottom edge of the collar [304].

13 November 1841 - All combatant ranks were given a new pattern **saber**, identical to that prescribed for Dragoon regiments (Illus. 872) [305].

8 April 1843 – Officers and lower ranks were given new **shakos** of the same size as received at this time by Dragoon regiments (Illus. 873). Along with this, in order to distinguish **rank** among the lower ranks, it was established that tape be sewn onto coat epaulettes and shoulder straps exactly as directed for Army Dragoon regiments [306].

10 May 1843 - Cover flaps for **cartridge pouches** were to be (with the cover sewn to the box): 4-1/2 vershoks [8 inches] long, 4-7/8 vershoks [9 inches] wide at the top edge, and 5-5/8 vershoks [10 inches] wide along the bottom edge [307].

2 January 1844 - Officers were to have a **cockade** on the band of the forage cap [308].

9 May 1844 - Shakos were replaced by **helmets** with plumes, of the same pattern and in accordance with the same directives as for Dragoon regiments (Illus. 874) [309].

4 January 1845 - Officers' **helmets** were to have a cockade on the right side under the chin-scales [310].

13 September 1846- New-pattern officers' **pistols** with percussion locks were introduced. Also approved were new carriers for them, described in detail in the chapter for Army Cuirassier regiments.

19 May 1847 – Lower ranks of the Instructional Cavalry Squadron were prescribed dark-green **forage caps** with red bands, with two dark-green lines of piping on the edges of the band and one line of red piping around the crown.

The following directives, laid out above for Dragoon regiments, were also applied in full to the Instructional Cavalry Squadron: **19 January 1848** – on firing-cap pouches on the cartridge pouches; **24 January 1848** – on deerskin sword belts of the pattern for His Royal Highness the Prince of Württemburg's Dragoon Regiment; **20 February 1848** – on officers' sword belts made from gold galloon; **25 April 1848** – on removal of the flap on the valise; **30 March 1851** – on cartridge-pouch crossbelts; **3 January 1852** – on covers for the firing nipples of percussion weapons; **18 February 1854** – on light-cavalry bridles; **29 April 1854** – on officers' campaign greatcoats.

INSTRUCTIONAL ARTILLERY BRIGADE [*Uchebnayaya Artilleriiskaya brigada.*]

11 February 1826 – Officers and lower ranks in the Instructional Artillery Brigade were prescribed single-breasted instead of double-breasted coats, with flat buttons, as were introduced at this time throughout the Army infantry and artillery, with red piping along the front opening and from the opening to the skirttails, and with red cuff flaps. Along with this change, long dark-green pants were also introduced, with red piping and black cloth **half-gaiters** [*polushtiblety*] (for company-grade officers only when in formation and on parade) buttoned with five or six small brass buttons. Generals, field-grade officers, and adjutants were prescribed boots with the **spurs** driven in.

Following the example throughout the Army infantry and artillery, in the Instructional Artillery Brigade the horizontal belt for the **knapsack** was ordered to be worn between two lower coat buttons, and the greatcoat was to be rolled into a tube inside a special oilskin case made of raven's-duck (Illus. 875) [311].

10 May 1826 - Generals, field-grade officers, and those company-grade officers who were by regulation mounted when in formation, were ordered during the summer to wear white linen **pants** without integral spats [*kozyrki*], of the same pattern as previously described for the dark-green ones (Illus. 876). In addition, suede [*zamshevyya*] pants of the same pattern were permitted to be worn instead of the linen pants [312].

1 January 1827 - Officers' **epaulettes** were to have small forged and stamped silver stars as rank distinctions, and of the same pattern and scheme as set forth above for all Army infantry and artillery [313].

14 February 1827 – **Cuff flaps** on officers' coats were ordered not to have red piping [314].

31 July 1827- Numbers and letters on the **covers** for shakos and pouches were ordered changed from yellow cloth to yellow [315].

24 March 1828 - The **coats** of lower ranks were forbidden to have cinches [316].

24 April 1828 – Officers and lower ranks were given new-pattern **shakos**, the same as received by Grenadier Artillery brigades but without a number on the grenade (Illus. 877). The width of the **crossbelt** and **swordbelt** was stipulated as 2 vershoks [3-1/2 inches], of the **knapsack shoulder belts**—1-1/2 vershoks [2-5/8 inches], and of the **belt across the chest**—1-1/8 vershoks [2 inches]. Black leather trim was added around **knapsacks**, which was prescribed to be 9 vershoks [15-3/4 inches] by 2-1/2 [4-3/8 inches] in breadth and width, and 8 vershoks [14 inches] high. The length of the cover from the upper edge was 6 vershoks [10-1/2 inches]. All noncombatant non-commissioned officers were given dark-green single-breasted **frock coats** with a single row of buttons and the same collar, cuffs, and shoulder straps as for combatant personnel. **Pants** were grey with red piping on the side seams. Non-combatant lower rank craftsmen [*masterovye*], as well as medical orderlies [*lazaretnye sluzhiteli*], with these same pants as just described for noncombant non-commissioned officers, were prescribed grey **jackets** [*kurtki*] modeled on the dress coat [317].

18 May 1829 - Non-commissioned officers who had been recommended by higher command for promotion to officer rank by virtue of years of service were permitted to have **silver sword-knots** [318].

16 December 1829- The black cuffs on officers' **frock coats** were changed to dark green, with red piping as before [319].

26 December 1829 - For all ranks the **buttons** on dress coats, frock coats, and greatcoats were prescribed to have the raised image of a grenade and two crossed cannons [320].

20 August 1830 – Officers' épées [*shpagi*] were replaced by **half-sabers** [*polusabli*] with black scabbards and gilded brass fittings (Illus. 8878) [321].

8 June 1832 – Officers were permitted to wear **moustaches** [322].

3 January 1833 - **Cloth half-gaiters** were abolished for company-grade officers and lower ranks, and **swordknots** (Illus. 879) were abolished except for those non-commissioned officers who had received them in silver [323].

20 February 1833 - All combatant ranks were given new-pattern **summer pants or trousers**, without buttons or integral spats (Illus. 880) [324].

28 March 1834 – New-pattern **short swords** with straight blades were confirmed, described above (see uniforms and weapons for Army Artillery) (Illus. 881) [325].

26 April 1834 – Numbers and letters for **shako covers** and **forage caps** were established: in Battery No. 1 Battery—1. B., in Battery No. 2 Battery—2. B., and in Light No. 1 Battery—1. L. The upper piping on forage caps in the 1st Battery Battery was prescribed to be red, in the 2nd Battery—white, and in the 1st Light Battery—dark blue. In all these batteries the upper and lower edges of the cap's band had red piping and yellow numbers and letters [326].

13 May 1834 – New-pattern **saddles** and **shabracks** for officers' riding horses were confirmed. The saddle was of black leather and the shabracks of dark-green cloth with black cloth stripes piped red along both sides. Surcingles were prescribed to be striped in black and red [327].

29 May 1834 - It was ordered that under no circumstances were officers to wear **knapsacks** when in formation. At all times they were to wear **spurs** and have straps on the pants to pass under the sole of the boot [328].

26 September 1834 - Lower ranks were directed to wear the **knapsack** on two belts lying crosswise on the chest (Illus. 881) [329].

20 August 1835 - It was ordered that for lower ranks a linen case or pocket for the forage cap was to be put on the outside of **knapsack** on the side that lay on the soldier's back. These cases were to be made from the linings of worn-out coats. For drummers the knapsack was to have one belt as before, worn over the left shoulder [330].

31 January 1836 - The lower ranks' **greatcoat** was to have nine buttons instead of ten: six along the front opening, two on the shoulder straps, and one on the flaps behind [331].

13 May 1836 – It was laid down that girths for officers' **saddles** were to be dark green with red stripes [332].

14 January 1837 - The wooden parts of the handles of **entrenching tools** were to be lacquered instead of painted with oil paints. The directives for the fitting and carrying of these tools were confirmed as laid out in detail above (see uniforms for Grenadier regiments [333].

15 July 1837 – Officers were given a new-pattern **sash** that had narrow silver lace instead of the previous wide lace, with three stripes of light-orange and black silk, and tied with its whole width between two lower coat buttons [334].

17 December 1837 – In order to introduce uniformity in officers' **epaulettes**, a new pattern was confirmed, having the addition of a fourth twist of thin braid [335].

4 January 1839 - Officers' **pants and trousers** were ordered not to have any bows or bands on the front, but were to be completely smooth in the manner established for lower ranks [336].

16 March 1839 - Lower ranks' **swordbelts**, at first 2-1/8 vershoks [3-3/4 inches] wide and then since 1828 2 vershoks [3-1/2 inches], were to be 1-1/2 vershoks [2-3/5 inches] wide. **Drummers' crossbelts** were left 2-1/2 vershoks [4-2/5 inches] wide as before [337].

23 January 1841 - The capes of officers' **greatcoats** were to be 1 arshin [28 inches] long as measured from the lower edge of the collar [338].

8 April 1843 – A new-pattern **shako** was confirmed, identical to that established for other troops (Illus. 882). Sewn-on tape was established for the shoulder straps of non-commissioned officers and corporals, described above in detail for Army Artillery) [339].

2 January 1844 – Officers' forage caps were to have an elongated metallic **cockade** on the band, in the same colors as prescribed for the cockades on officers' hats [340].

9 May 1844 – For all combatant ranks in the Instructional Artillery Brigade shakos were replaced by **helmets** with plumes, identical to those confirmed for Grenadier Artillery brigades but with the previous plate (Illus. 883) [341].

20 May 1844 – Approval was given to a new scheme for differentiating the **forage caps** of lower ranks. Based on this the piping around the upper crown was prescribed to be of red cloth, while the band was black cloth with red piping along both edges and the cut-out battery number and letter backed by yellow cloth. Officers' cap bands were the same as lower ranks' but, as before, without numbers or letters (342).

4 January 1845 - Officers' **helmets** were to have a cockade on the right side under the chin-scales, following the pattern of the cockade on hats (343).

9 August 1845 – When in camp uniform **helmets** were ordered to be worn without plumes even though the personnel under direction to wear them were in dress coats (344).

In addition to the changes for the Instructional Artillery Brigade presented above, the following directives for Army Artillery were also applied with equal force: **19 May 1847** – on lower ranks' forage caps; **9 January 1848** – on the uniform for walking out on designated holidays; **14 September 1849** – on percussion pistols; **9 and 25 November 1849** – on fitting the helmet; **17 January 1851** – on the manner of taking up the greatcoat skirts; **20 August 1851** – on items in the knapsack; **26 January 1852** – on noncombatant lower ranks' forage caps; **3 January 1853** – on frock coats for noncombatant lower ranks; **18 February 1854** – on light-cavalry horse furniture; **29 April 1854** – on officers' campaign greatcoats.

INSTRUCTIONAL SAPPER BATTALION [*Uchebnyi Sapernyi batal'on.*]

11 February 1826 – Officers and lower ranks in the Instructional Sapper Battalion were prescribed single-breasted instead of double-breasted coats, with flat buttons, as were introduced at this time throughout the Army infantry, artillery, and sapper and pioneer battalions, with red piping along the front opening and from the opening to the skirttails, and with red cuff flaps. Along with this change, long dark-green pants were also introduced, with red piping and black cloth **half-gaiters** [*polushtiblety*] (for company-grade officers only when in formation and on parade) buttoned with five or six small brass buttons. The general, field-grade officers, and adjutant were prescribed boots with the **spurs** driven in. Following the example of all other infantry troops, in the Instructional Sapper Battalion the horizontal belt for the **knapsack** was ordered to be worn between two lower coat buttons, and the greatcoat was to be rolled into a tube inside a special oilskin case made of raven's-duck (Illus. 884) (345).

10 May 1826 – The general, field-grade officers, and those company-grade officers who were by regulation mounted when in formation, were ordered during the summer to wear white linen **pants** without integral spats [*kozyrki*], of the same pattern as previously described for the dark-green ones (Illus. 885). In addition, suede [*zamshevyya*] pants of the same pattern were permitted to be worn instead of the linen pants (346).

1 January 1827 - Officers' **epaulettes** were to have small forged and stamped gold stars as rank distinctions, of the same pattern and scheme as set forth above for Army Sapper and Pioneer battalions (347).

14 February 1827 – Cuff flaps on officers' coats were ordered not to have red piping (348).

31 July 1827- Numbers and letters on the **covers** for shakos and pouches were ordered changed from yellow cloth to yellow (349).

4 March 1828 - The **coats** of lower ranks were forbidden to have cinches (350).

24 April 1828 – Officers and lower ranks were given new-pattern **shakos**, the same as received by the Army Sapper battalion (Illus. 886). The width of the **crossbelt** and **swordbelt** was stipulated as 2 vershoks [3-1/2 inches], of the **knapsack shoulder belts**—1-1/2 vershoks [2-5/8 inches], and of the **belt across the chest**—1-1/8 vershoks [2 inches]. Black leather trim was added around **knapsacks**, which was prescribed to be 9 vershoks [15-3/4 inches] by 2-1/2 [4-3/8] in breadth and width, and 8 vershoks [14 inches] high. The length of the cover (from the upper edge) was 6 vershoks [10-1/2 inches]. All noncombatant non-commissioned officers were given dark-green single-breasted **frock coats** with a single row of buttons and the same collar, cuffs, and shoulder straps as for combatant personnel. **Pants** were grey with red piping on the side seams. Non-combatant lower rank craftsmen [*masterovye*], as well as medical orderlies [*lazaretnye sluzhiteli*], with these same pants as just described for noncombant non-commissioned officers, were prescribed grey **jackets** [*kurtki*] modeled on the dress coat (351).

16 December 1829- The black cuffs on officers' **frock coats** were changed to dark green, with red piping as before (352).

26 December 1829 - For all ranks the **buttons** on dress coats, frock coats, and greatcoats were prescribed to have the raised image of a grenade, two crossed axes, and the upright Cyrillic letter U (353).

20 August 1830 – Officers' épées [*shpagi*] were replaced by **half-sabers** [*polusabli*] identical to those introduced for all other army foot troops (Illus. 8878) (354).

8 June 1832 – Officers were permitted to wear **moustaches** (355).

3 January 1833 - **Cloth half-gaiters** were abolished for company-grade officers and lower ranks, and **swordknots** (Illus. 887) were only kept for those non-commissioned officers who had received them in silver (356).

20 February 1833 - All combatant ranks were given new-pattern **summer pants or trousers**, without buttons or integral spats (Illus. 888) (357).

28 March 1834 – New-pattern **short swords** with straight blades were confirmed, as described above under uniforms and weapons for Army Artillery (Illus. 889) [358].

26 September 1834 - Lower ranks were directed to wear the **knapsack** on two belts lying crosswise on the chest (Illus. 889)[359].

20 August 1835 – Officers were ordered to wear **knapsacks** using only two lacquered shoulder straps, without any horizontal belt across the chest (Illus. 890). For lower ranks, it was ordered that a linen case or pocket for the forage cap was to be put on the outside of **knapsack** on the side that lay on the soldier's back. These cases were to be made from the linings of worn-out coats. For drummers the knapsack was to have one belt as before, worn over the left shoulder [360].

31 January 1836 - The lower ranks' **greatcoat** was to have nine buttons instead of ten: six along the front opening, two on the shoulder straps, and one on the flaps behind [361].

27 April 1836 – It was ordered that shako **pompons** be lined with black leather [362].

13 May 1836 – It was laid down that girths for officers' **saddles** were to be dark green with red stripes [363].

14 January 1837 - The wooden parts of the handles of **entrenching tools** were to be lacquered instead of painted with oil paints. The directives for the fitting and carrying of these tools were confirmed as laid out in detail above for uniforms for Grenadier regiments [364].

15 July 1837 – Officers were given a new-pattern **sash** that had narrow silver lace instead of the previous wide lace, with three stripes of light-orange and black silk, and tied with its whole width between two lower coat buttons [365].

17 December 1837 – In order to introduce uniformity in officers' **epaulettes**, a new pattern was confirmed, having the addition of a fourth twist of thin braid [366].

4 January 1839 - Officers' **pants and trousers** were ordered not to have any bows or bands on the front, but were to be completely smooth in the manner established for lower ranks [367].

16 March 1839 - Lower ranks' **swordbelts**, at first 2-1/8 vershoks [3-3/4 inches] wide and then—since 1828—2 vershoks [3-1/2 inches], were to be 1-1/2 vershoks [2-3/5 inches] wide. **Drummers' crossbelts** were left 2-1/2 vershoks [4-2/5 inches] wide as before [368].

23 January 1841 - The capes of officers' **greatcoats** were to be 1 arshin [28 inches] long as measured from the lower edge of the collar [369].

8 April 1843 – A new-pattern **shako** was confirmed, identical to that established for other troops (Illus. 891). Sewn-on tape was established for the **shoulder straps** of non-commissioned officers and corporals, described above in detail for Grenadier regiments [370].

2 January 1844 – Officers' forage caps were to have an elongated metallic **cockade** on the band, in the same colors as prescribed for the cockades on officers' hats [371].

9 May 1844 – Instad of shakos, all combatant ranks in the Instructional Sapper Battalion shakos were given **helmets** with plumes, of the same patterns as confirmed for Grenadier regiments but with the previous plate and white fittins (Illus. 892) [372].

20 May 1844 – Approval was given to a new scheme for differentiating the **forage caps** of lower ranks. Based on this the piping around the upper crown was prescribed to be of red cloth, while the band was black cloth with red piping along both edges and had the cut-out company number and letter backed by yellow cloth. Officers' cap bands were the same as lower ranks' but, as before, without numbers or letters [373].

4 January 1845 - Officers' **helmets** were to have a cockade on the right side under the chin-scales, as described above for the Instructional Artillery Brigade [374].

9 August 1845 – When in camp uniform **helmets** were ordered to be worn without plumes even though the personnel prescribed them were in dress coats [375].

In addition to the changes for the Instructional Sapper Battalion presented above, the following directives for Sapper battalions were also applied with equal force: **23 June 1846** – on fitting firing-cap pouches; **9 January 1848** – on the uniform for walking out on designated holidays; **19 April 1849** – on English signal bugles; **14 September 1849** – on percussion pistols; **9 and 25 November 1849** – on fitting the helmet; **24 December 1849** – on half-sabers awarded for bravery; **17 January 1851** – on the manner of taking up the greatcoat skirts; **8 July 1851** – on frizzen covers being withdrawn; **20 August 1851** – on items in the knapsack; **26 January 1852** – on noncombatant lower ranks' forage caps; **3 January 1853** – on frock coats for noncombatant lower ranks; **18 February 1854** – on valises for the saddles; **29 April 1854** – on officers' campaign greatcoats; **13 February 1855** – on fitting firing-cap pouches.

NOTES

(1) *Collection of Laws and Regulations*, 1826, Book I, pgs. 105-110.
(2) Ibid., Book II, pg. 47.
(3) Ibid., Book III, pg. 255.
(4) Ibid., Book IV, pg. 95.
(5) Ibid., 1827, Book I, pg. 3.
(6) Ibid., pg. 153.
(7) Ibid., Book III, pg. 89.
(8) Ibid., Book IV, pg. 267.
(9) Ibid., pg. 257.
(10) Ibid., 1828, Book I, pg. 211.
(11) Ibid., Book II, pg. 131 et seq.
(12) Ibid., 1828, Book II, pg. 221, §12.
(13) Ibid., Book IV, pg. 107.
(14) Ibid., pg. 115, and information received from the War Ministry's Commissariat Department.
(15) *Collection of Laws and Regulations*, 1832, Book II, pg. 545.
(16) Ibid., 1833, Book I, pg. 419.
(17) Ibid., pg. 463.
(18) Ibid., pg. 465.
(19) Information received from the War Ministry's Artillery Department, and HIGHEST Confirmed model short-sword.
(20) *Collection of Laws and Regulations*, 1834, Book III, pg. 465.
(21) Ibid., 1835, Book III, pg. 179.
(22) Ibid., 1836, Book I, pg. 137.
(23) Information received from the War Ministry's Commissariat Department.
(24) *Collection of Laws and Regulations*, 1836, Book II, pg. 171.
(25) Ibid., 137, Book I, pg. 353.
(26) Ibid., Book III, pg. 47.
(27) Ibid., Book IV, pg. 325.
(28) Ibid., 1838, Book I, pg. 19.
(29) Ibid., 1839, Book I, pg. 3.
(30) Ibid., pg. 179.
(31) Order of the Minister of War, 16 October 1840, No. 60.
(32) Ditto, 23 January 1841, No. 8.
(33) Ditto, 8 April 1843, Nos. 44 and 46.
(34) Ditto, 10 May 1843, No. 63.
(35) Ditto, 2 January 1844, No. 1.
(36) Ditto, 9 May 1844, Nos. 63 and 64.
(37) Ditto, 20 May 1844, No. 69.
(38) Ditto, 17 November 1844, No. 138.
(39) Ditto, 4 January 1845, No. 1.
(40) Ditto, 9 August 1845, No. 101.
(41) Ditto, 8 March 1847, No. 46.
(42) Ditto, 19 May 1847, No. 86.
(43) Ditto, 29 November 1847, No. 186.
(44) Ditto, 9 January 1848, No. 8.
(45) Ditto, 19 April 1849, No. 31.
(46) Ditto, 14 September 1849, No. 88.
(47) Ditto, 9 and 23 November 1849, Nos. 110 and 117.
(48) Ditto, 24 December 1849, No. 133.
(49) Ditto, 17 January 1851, No. 7.
(50) Ditto, 13 December 1851, No. 133.
(51) Ditto, 20 October 1851, No. 120.
(52) Ditto, 26 January 1852, No. 15.
(53) Ditto, 28 December 1852, No. 147.
(54) Ditto, 3 January 1853, No. 3.
(55) Ditto, 18 Feb 1854, No. 21.
(56) Ditto, 29 April 1854, No. 53.
(57) Ditto, 13 Feb 1855, No. 28.
(58) *Collection of Laws and Regulations*, 1826, Book I, pgs. 108-110.
(59) Ibid., Book III, pg. 255.
(60) Ibid., 1827, Book I, pg. 3.
(61) Ibid., Book III, pg. 89.
(62) Information received from the War Ministry's Commissariat Department.
(63) *Collection of Laws and Regulations*, 1827, Book IV, pgs. 17-19.
(64) Ibid., pg. 257.
(65) Ibid., pg. 211.
(66) Ibid., pg. 131.
(67) Ibid., 1828, Book II, pgs. 131 et seq.
(68) Information received from the War Ministry's Commissariat Department.
(69) *Collection of Laws and Regulations*, 1829, Book III, pg. 5.
(70) Ibid., Book IV, pg. 107.
(71) Ibid., pg. 115.
(72) Information received from the War Ministry's Commissariat Department.
(73) From the files of the War Ministry's Commissariat Dep.
(74) *Collection of Laws and Regulations*, 1834, Book II, pgs. 245-247.
(75) Ibid., Book III, pg. 433.
(76) Ibid., Book IV, pg. 257.
(77) Ibid., 1835, Book I, pg. 317.
(78) Ibid., Book II, pg. 283.
(79) Ibid., 1836, Book I, pg. 137.
(80) Ibid., Book II, pg. 171.
(81) Ibid., Book IV, pgs. 153 and 154.
(82) Ibid., 1837, Book I, pgs. 133.
(83) Ibid., pg. 55.
(84) Ibid., Book III, pg. 47.
(85) Ibid., Book IV, pg. 325.
(86) Ibid., 1838, Book I, pgs. 311-315.
(87) Ibid., pg. 329.
(88) Ibid., 1839, Book I, pg. 3.
(89) Order of the Minister of War, 16 October 1840, No. 60.
(90) Ditto, 23 January 1841, No. 8.
(91) Information received from the War Ministry's Artillery Department, and HIGHEST Confirmed model saber.
(92) Order of the Minister of War, 8 April 1843, Nos. 44 and 46.
(93) Ditto, 10 May 1843, No. 63.
(94) Ditto, 2 January 1844, No. 1.
(95) Ditto, 9 May 1844, Nos. 63 and 64.
(96) Ditto, 21 September 1844, No. 115.
(97) Ditto, 4 January 1845, No. 1.
(98) Ditto, 9 August 1845, No. 101.
(99) Ditto, 31 March 1846, No. 58.
(100) Ditto, 7 August 1846, No. 138.
(101) Ditto, 13 September 1846, No. 160.
(102) Ditto, 19 May 1847, No. 86.
(103) Ditto, 31 August 1847, No. 145, and memorandum of the Minister of War to HIS IMPERIAL HIGHNESS the Commander-in-Chief of the Guards and Grenadier Corps, 5 November 1847, No. 10047.
(104) Order of the Minister of War, 9 January 1848, No. 8.
(105) Ditto, 19 January 1848, No. 17.
(106) Ditto, 25 April 1848, No. 80.
(107) Ditto, 9 and 25 November 1849, Nos. 110 and 117.
(108) Ditto, 24 December 1849, No. 133.
(109) Ditto, 5 March 1850, No. 18.

(110) Ditto, 30 March 1851, No. 36.
(111) Ditto, 15 April 1851, No. 46.
(112) Ditto, 3 January 1852, No. 2.
(113) Ditto, 26 January 1852, No. 15.
(114) Ditto, 13 August 1853, No. 61.
(115) Ditto, 15 November 1853, No. 78.
(116) Ditto, 29 April 1854, No. 53.
(117) *Collection of Laws and Regulations*, 1826, Book I, pg. 105.
(118) Ibid., Book III, pg. 161.
(119) Ibid., pg. 197.
(120) Ibid., 1827, Book I, pg. 3.
(121) Ibid., 1829, Book IV, pg. 107.
(122) Ibid., pg. 115.
(123) Ibid., 1832, Book II, pg. 545.
(124) Ibid., 1837, Book III, pg. 47.
(125) Ibid., Book IV, pg. 325.
(126) Ibid., 1839, Book I, pg. 3.
(127) Order of the Minister of War, 23 January 1841, No. 8.
(128) Ditto, 2 January 1844, No. 1.
(129) Ditto, 2 February 1846, No. 26.
(130) Ditto, 13 October 1849, No. 104.
(131) Ditto, 24 December 1849, No. 133.
(132) *Collection of Laws and Regulations*, 1826, Book I, pg. 105, and statements from contemporaries who served at that time in the Guards General Staff.
(133) *Collection of Laws and Regulations*, 1826, Book III, pg. 161.
(134) Ibid., pg. 197.
(135) Ibid., 1829, Book IV, pg. 115.
(136) Ibid., 1831, Book I, pg. 58.
(137) Order of the Minister of War, 7 December 1844, No. 147.
(138) Ditto, 4 January 1845, No. 1.
(139) Ditto, 14 September 1849, No. 88.
(140) Ditto, 13 October 1849, No. 104.
(141) Ditto, 24 December 1849, No. 133.
(142) Ditto, 18 February 1854, No. 21.
(143) Ditto, 29 April 1854, No. 53.
(144) *Collection of Laws and Regulations*, 1826, Book I, pgs. 105 to 110.
(145) Ibid., Book II, pg. 47.
(146) Ibid., Book III, pg. 255.
(147) Ibid., Book IV, pg. 95.
(148) Ibid., 1827, Book I, pg. 3.
(149) Ibid., Book III, pg. 89.
(150) Ibid., Book IV, pg. 257.
(151) Ibid., 1828, Book I, pg. 211.
(152) Ibid., Book II, pgs. 131 et seq.
(153) Ibid., 1829, Book II, pg. 221, § 12.
(154) Ibid., Book IV, pg. 115, and information received from the War Ministry's Commissariat Department.
(155) *Collection of Laws and Regulations*, 1832, Book II, pg. 545.
(156) Ibid., 1833, Book I, pg. 419.
(157) Ibid., pg. 463.
(158) Information received from the War Ministry's Commissariat Department.
(159) *Collection of Laws and Regulations*, 1834, Book III, pg. 465.
(160) Ibid., 1835, Book III, pg. 179.
(161) Ibid., 1836, Book I, pg. 137.
(162) Information received from the War Ministry's Commissariat Department.
(163) *Collection of Laws and Regulations*, 1836, Book II, pg. 171.
(164) Ibid., Book IV, pg. 157.
(165) Ibid., 1837, Book I, pg. 353.
(166) Ibid., Book III, pg. 47.
(167) Ibid., Book IV, pg. 325.
(168) Ibid., 1839, Book I, pg. 3.
(169) Ibid., pg. 179.
(170) Order of the Minister of War, 16 October 1840, No. 60.
(171) Ditto, 23 January 1841, No. 8.
(172) Ditto, 8 April 1843, Nos. 44, 46, and 47.
(173) Ditto, 10 May 1843, No. 63.
(174) Ditto, 2 January 1844, No. 1.
(175) Ditto, 9 May 1844, Nos. 63 and 64.
(176) Ditto, 20 May 1844, No. 69.
(177) Ditto, 17 November 1844, No. 138.
(178) Ditto, 4 January 1845, No. 1.
(179) *Collection of Laws and Regulations*, 1826, Book I, pgs. 105 et seq.
(180) Ibid., Book IV, pg. 95.
(181) Ibid., 1828, Book II, pgs. 131 et seq.
(182) Information received from the War Ministry's Commissariat Dep.
(183) *Collection of Laws and Regulations*, 1833, Book I, pg. 419.
(184) Ibid., pg. 463.
(185) Order of the Minister of War, 8 April 1843, Nos. 44, 46, and 47.
(186) Ditto, 9 May 1844, Nos. 63 and 64.
(187) Ditto, 4 January 1845, No. 1.
(188) *Collection of Laws and Regulations*, 1826, Book I, pgs. 105 et seq.
(189) Ibid., Book III, pg. 255.
(190) Ibid., 1827, Book I, pg. 3.
(191) *Complete Collection of Laws of the Russian Empire* [*Polnoe Sobranie Zakonov*, henceforth PSZ], Second collection, Vol. II, pg. 587, No. 1222.
(192) *Collection of Laws and Regulations*, 1827, Book III, pg. 89.
(193) Ibid., Book IV, pg. 257.
(194) Ibid., 1828, Book I, pg. 211.
(195) Information received from the War Ministry's Commissariat Dep.
(196) *Collection of Laws and Regulations*, 1828, Book II, pgs. 131 et seq., and information received from the War Ministry's Commissariat Dep.
(197) PSZ, Second collection, Vol. V, pg. 28, No. 3425.
(198) Ibid., pg. 621, No. 3725.
(199) Ibid., pg. 149, No. 4005.
(200) Ibid., pg. 248, No. 4064.
(201) Ibid., pg. 407, No. 4120.
(202) Ibid., pg. 498, No. 4188, §2.
(203) *Collection of Laws and Regulations*, 1832, Book II, pg. 545.
(204) Ibid., 1833, Book I, pg. 419.
(205) Ibid., pg. 435.
(206) Ibid., 1834, Book III, pg. 465.
(207) Ibid., 1835, Book III, pg. 179.
(208) Ibid., 1836, Book I, pg. 137.
(209) Information received from the War Ministry's Commissariat Dep.
(210) *Collection of Laws and Regulations*, 1836, Book II, pg. 171.
(211) Ibid., 1837, Book IV, pg. 325.
(212) Ibid., 1839, Book I, pg. 3.
(213) Ibid., pg. 179.
(214) Order of the Minister of War, 16 October 1840, No. 60.
(215) Ditto, 23 January 1841, No. 8.
(216) Ditto, 8 April 1843, Nos. 44, 46, and 47.
(217) Ditto, 10 May 1843, No. 63.
(218) Ditto, 2 January 1844, No. 1.
(219) Order of the Duty General of the Main Naval Staff, 5 May 1844, No. 644.
(220) Information received from the Guards Équipage.
(221) Order of the Minister of War, 4 January 1845, No. 1.
(222) Ditto, 9 January 1848, No. 8.
(223) Ditto, 24 December 1849, No. 133.
(224) Ditto, 28 December 1852, No. 147.

(225) Ditto, 29 April 1854, No. 53.
(226) *Collection of Laws and Regulations*, 1826, Book I, pgs. 105 and 125.
(227) Ibid., Book II, pg. 47.
(228) Order of the Chief of HIS IMPERIAL MAJESTY'S Main Staff, 22 October 1826, No. 9.
(229) *Collection of Laws and Regulations*, 1827, Book I, pg. 3.
(230) Ibid., Book III, pg. 89.
(231) Ibid., pg. 211.
(232) Ibid., 1828, Book II, pgs. 131 et seq.
(233) Ibid., 1829, Book II, pg. 221, § 12.
(234) Ibid., pg. 115.
(235) Ibid., 1830, Book III, pg. 179.
(236) Ibid., 1832, Book II, pg. 545.
(237) Ibid., 1833, Book I, pg. 419.
(238) *Collection of Laws and Regulations Relating to the Military Administration*, 1833, Book I, pg. 463, and information received from the War Ministry's Commissariat Department.
(239) *Collection of Laws and Regulations*, 1833, Book I, pg. 463.
(240) From the files of the War Ministry's Commissariat Department.
(241) *Collection of Laws and Regulations Relating to the Military Administration*, 1834, Book I, pg. 46, § 9, and information received from the War Ministry's Commissariat Department.
Collection of Laws and Regulations, 1834, Book III, pg. 465.
(243) Ibid., 1835, Book II, pg. 9, § 2, and information received from the War Ministry's Commissariat Department.
(244) *Collection of Laws and Regulations*, 1835, Book III, pg. 179.
(245) Ibid., 1836, Book I, pg. 137.
(246) Ibid., Book II, pg. 171.
(247) Ibid., pg. 209.
(248) Ibid., Book IV, pg. 157.
(249) Ibid., 1837, Book I, pg. 353.
(250) Ibid., Book III, pg. 47.
(251) Ibid., Book IV, pg. 325.
(252) Ibid., 1838, Book I, pg. 19.
(253) Ibid., 1839, Book I, pg. 3.
(254) Ibid., pg. 179.
(255) Order of the Minster of War, 23 January 1841, No. 8.
(256) Ditto, 8 April 1843, Nos. 44, 46, and 47.
(257) Ditto, 10 May 1843, No. 63.
(258) Ditto, 8 January 1844, No. 3.
(259) Ditto, 9 May 1844, Nos. 63 and 64.
(260) Ditto, 4 January 1845, No. 1.
(261) Ditto, 9 August 1845, No. 101.
(262) *Collection of Laws and Regulations*, 1826, Book I, pgs. 108-110.
(263) Ibid., Book II, pg. 75.
(264) Ibid., 1827, Book I, pg. 3.
(265) Ibid., Book II, pg. 169.
(266) Ibid., Book III, pg. 89.
(267) Information received from the War Ministry's Commissariat Department.
(268) *Collection of Laws and Regulations*, 1827, Book IV, pgs. 17-19.
(269) Ibid., pgs. 157-159, and information received from the War Ministry's Commissariat Department.
(270) Ibid., 1828, Book I, pg. 131, and HIGHEST Confirmed models preserved by the War Ministry's Commissariat Department.
(271) *Collection of Laws and Regulations*, 1828, Book II, pgs. 131 et seq.

(272) Ibid., Book IV, pg. 47.
(273) Ibid., pg. 107.
(274) From the files of the War Ministry's Commissariat Department.
(275) Ditto.
(276) *Collection of Laws and Regulations*, 1830, Book III pg. 217.
(277) From the files of the War Ministry's Commissariat Department.
(278) *Collection of Laws and Regulations*, 1832, Book III pg. 329.
(279) Ibid., pg. 485.
(280) Ibid., pg. 487.
(281) From the files of the War Ministry's Commissariat Department.
(282) Information received from the War Ministry's Commissariat Department.
(283) *Collection of Laws and Regulations*, 1834, Book II pg. 233.
(284) Ibid., pg. 237.
(285) Ibid., pgs. 245-247.
(286) Ibid., pg. 209.
(287) Ibid., Book IV, pg. 141.
(288) Ibid., pg. 257.
(289) Ibid., 1835, Book I, pg. 137.
(290) Ibid., pg. 367.
(291) Ibid., Book II, pg. 283.
(292) Ibid., Book III, pg. 175-178.
(293) Ibid., Book IV, pg. 55.
(294) Ibid., 1836, Book I, pg. 137-139.
(295) Ibid., Book II, pg. 171.
(296) Ibid., pg. 173.
(297) Ibid., Book IV, pg. 153 and 154.
(298) Ibid., 1837, Book I., pg. 133.
(299) Ibid., pg. 55.
(300) Ibid., Book III, pg. 47.
(301) Ibid., Book IV., pg. 325.
(302) Ibid., 1838, Book I, pg. 329.
(303) Ibid., 1839, Book I, pg. 3.
(304) Order of the Minister of War, 23 January 1841, No. 8.
(305) Information received from the War Ministry's Artillery Departmen, and HIGHEST Confirmed models sabers.
(306) Order of the Minister of War, 8 April 1843, Nos. 66 and 67.
(307) Ibid., 10 May 1843, No. 63.
(308) Ibid., 2 January 1844, No. 1.
(309) Ibid., 9 May 1844, Nos. 63 and 64.
(310) Ibid., 4 January 1845, No. 1.
(311) *Collection of Laws and Regulations*, 1826, Book I, pgs. 105 and 125.
(312) Ibid., Book II, pg. 47.
(313) Ibid., Book III, pg. 255.
(314) Ibid., pg. 153.
(315) Ibid., pg. 89.
(316) Ibid., 1828, Book I, pg. 211.
(317) Ibid., Book II, pgs. 131 et seq.
(318) Ibid., 1829, Book II, pgs. 221, § 12.
(319) Ibid., pg. 107.
(320) Ibid., pg. 115.
(321) Ibid., 1830, Book III, pg. 179.
(322) Ibid., 1832, Book II, pg. 545.
(323) Ibid., 1833, Book I, pg. 419.
(324) Ibid., pg. 463, and information received from the War Ministry's Commissariat Department.
(325) Information received from the War Ministry's Artillery Department, and a HIGHEST Confirmed model short-sword.

(326) *Collection of Laws and Regulations*, 1834, Book II, pg. 243.
(327) Ibid., pg. 257.
(328) Ibid., pg. 163.
(329) Ibid., Book III, pg. 465.
(330) Ibid., 1835, Book III, pg. 179.
(331) Ibid., 1836, Book I, pg. 137.
(332) Ibid. Book II, pg. 209.
(333) Ibid., 1837, Book I, pg. 353.
(334) Ibid., Book III, pg. 47.
(335) Ibid., 1837, Book IV, pg. 325.
(336) Ibid., 1839, Book I, pg. 3.
(337) Ibid., pg. 179.
(338) Order of the Minister or War, 23 January 1841, No. 8.
(339) Ditto, 8 April 1843, No. 46.
(340) Ditto, 2 January 1844 No. 1.
(341) Ditto, 9 May 1844, Nos. 63 and 64.
(342) Ditto, 20 May 1844, No. 69.
(343) Ditto, 4 January 1845, No. 1.
(344) Ditto, 4 August 1845, No. 101.
(345) *Collection of Laws and Regulations*, 1826, Book I, pgs. 105 and 125.
(346) Ibid., Book II, pg. 47.
(347) Ibid., Book III, pg. 255.
(348) Ibid., pg. 153.
(349) Ibid., pg. 89.
(350) Ibid., 1828, Book I, pg. 211.
(351) Ibid., Book II, pgs. 131 et seq.
(352) Ibid., pg. 107.
(353) Ibid., pg. 115.
(354) Ibid., 1830, Book III, pg. 179.
(355) Ibid., 1832, Book II, pg. 545.
(356) Ibid., 1833, Book I, pg. 419.
(357) Ibid., pg. 463, and information received from the War Ministry's Commissariat Department.
(358) Information received from the War Ministry's Artillery Department, and a HIGHEST Confirmed model short-sword.
(359) *Collection of Laws and Regulations*, 1834, Book II, pg. 465.
(360) Ibid., 1835, Book III, pg. 179.
(361) Ibid., 1836, Book I, pg. 137.
(362) Ibid., Book II, pg. 171.
(363) Ibid. Book II, pg. 209.
(364) Ibid., 1837, Book I, pg. 353.
(365) Ibid., Book III, pg. 47.
(366) Ibid., Book IV, pg. 325.
(367) Ibid., 1839, Book I, pg. 3.
(368) Ibid., pg. 179.
(369) Order of the Minister of War, 23 January 1841, No. 8.
(370) Ditto, 8 April 1843, No. 46.
(371) Ditto, 2 January 1844 No. 1.
(372) Ditto, 9 May 1844, Nos. 63 and 64.
(373) Ditto, 20 May 1844, No. 69.
(374) Ditto, 4 January 1845, No. 1.
(375) Ditto, 4 August 1845, No. 101.

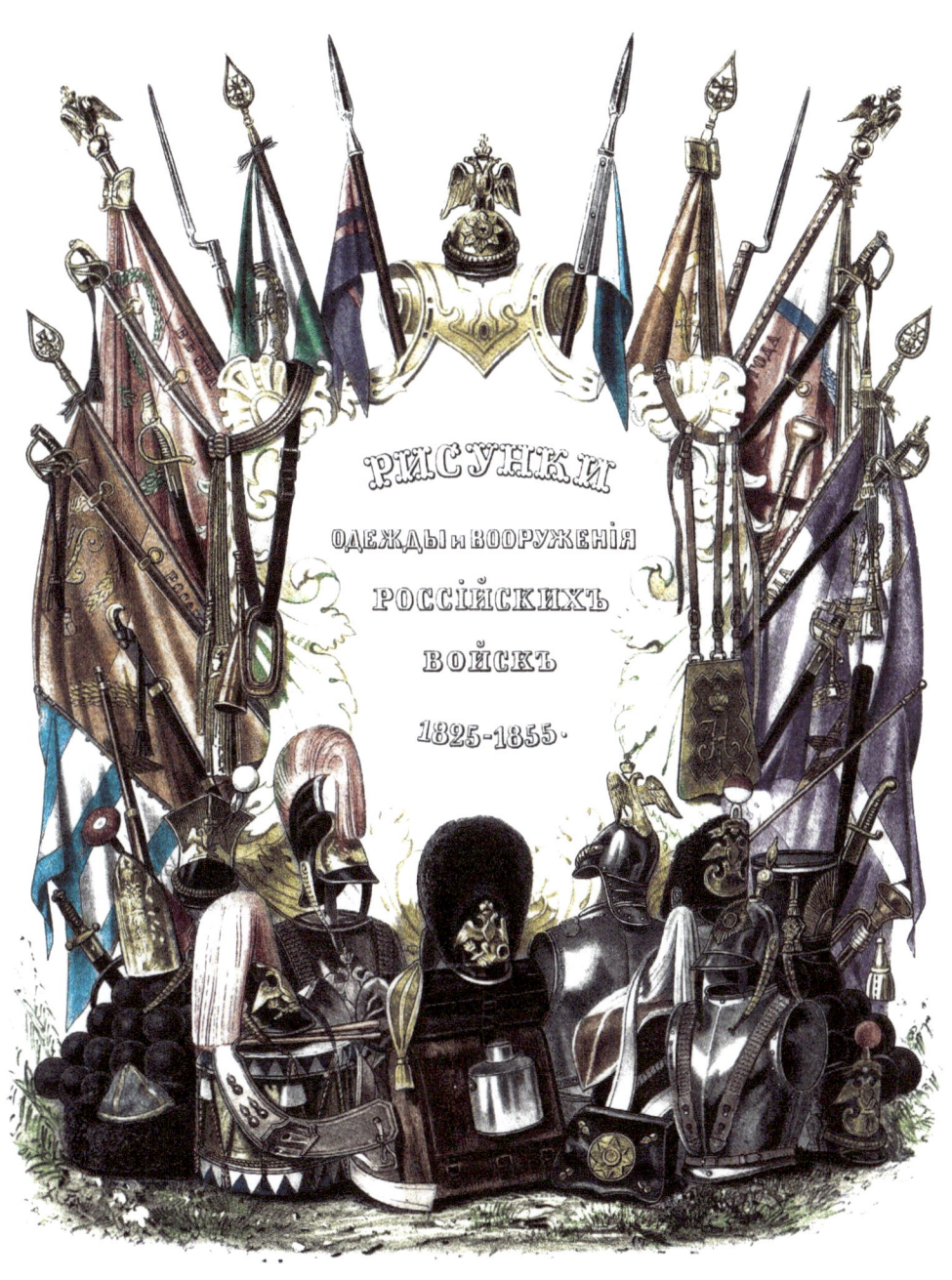

PLATES LIST OF ILLUSTRATIONS

796. Non-Commissioned Officer and Company-Grade Officer. L.-Gds. Sapper Battalion, 1826-1828.
797. Adjutant. L.-Gds. Sapper Battalion, 1826-1828.
798. Hornist and Company-Grade Officer. L.-Gds. Sapper Battalion, 1828-1833.
799. Company-Grade Officer. L.-Gds. Sapper Battalion, 1833.
800. Drummer. L.-Gds. Sapper Battalion, 1834-43.
801. Non-Commissioned Officer. L.-Gds. Sapper Battalion, 1834-1843.
802. Private. L.-Gds. Sapper Battalion, 1843-1844.
803. Non-Commissioned Officer and Musician. L.-Gds. Sapper Battalion, 1844-1849.
804. Company-Grade Officer. L.-Gds. Sapper Battalion, 1845-1849.
805. Non-Commissioned Officer. L.-Gds. Horse-Pioneer Squadron, 1827-1829.
806. NCO and Company-Grade Officer. L.-Gds. Horse-Pioneer Squadron, 1829-1841.
807. Trumpeter. L.-Gds. Horse-Pioneer Squadron, 1841-1843.
808. Trumpeter and Field-Grade Officer. L.-Gds. Horse-Pioneer Squadron, 1843-1849. *Note:* On 28 September 1845 the L.-Gds. Horse-Pioneer Squadron was renamed a battalion [*divizion*].
809. Field-Grade Officer. L.-Gds. Horse-Pioneer Battalion, 1845-1849.
810. Private. L.-Gds. Horse-Pioneer Battalion, 1846-1855.
811. Company-Grade Officer. Guards Engineers, 1826-1846.
812. Field-Grade Officer. Guards Engineers, 1826-1846.
813. Field-Grade Officer. Guards Engineers, 1846-1849.
814. Field-Grade Officer. Guards General Staff, 1826-1844.
815. Company-Grade Officer. Guards General Staff, 1826-1844.
816. Generals. Guards General Staff, 1844.
817. Field-Grade Officer. Guards General Staff, 1845-1849.
818. Company-Grade Officer. Guards General Staff, 1849-1855.
819. Non-Commissioned Officer and Private. L.-Gds. Garrison Battalion, 1826-1828.
820. Company-Grade Officer. L.-Gds. Garrison Battalion, 1826-1828.
821. Drummer and Field-Grade Officer L.-Gds. Garrison Battalion, 1826-1828.
822. Drummer and Company-Grade Officer. L.-Gds. Garrison Battalion, 1828-1833.
823. Non-Commissioned Officer. L.-Gds. Garrison Battalion, 1833-1843.
824. Company-Grade Officer. L.-Gds. Garrison Battalion, 1833-1843.
825. Private. L.-Gds. Garrison Battalion, 1834-1843.
826. Musician and Non-Commissioned Officer. L.-Gds. Garrison Battalion, 1844-1849.
827. Company-Grade Officer and Private. Guards Invalid Companies, 1826-1828.
828. Non-Commissioned Officer. Guards Invalid Companies, 1828-1833.
829. Private. Guards Invalid No. 16 Company, 1832-1833.
830. Non-Commissioned Officer. Guards Invalid No. 16 Company, 1833-1838.
831. Private. Guards Invalid Companies, 1833-1843.
832. Company-Grade Officer. Guards Invalid Companies, 1843-1844.
833. Private. Guards Invalid Companies, 1844-1845.
834. Company-Grade Officer. Guards Invalid Companies, 1845-1849.
835. Private, Guards Équipage. Cannoneer, Guards Équipage Artillery Command. Non-Commissioned Officer, Guards Barge Company. 1826-1828.
836. Company-Grade Officers. Guards Équipage and its Artillery Command, 1826-1828.
837. Company-Grade Officers. Guards Barge Company, 1827-1828.
838. Bombardier and Company-Grade Officer. Guards Équipage Artillery Company, 1828-1830.
839. Drummer, Guards Équipage, and Private, Guards Barge Company. 1828-1830.
840. Clerk. Guards Équipage, 1828-1830.
841. Company-Grade Officer. Guards Barge Company, 1830-1843.

842. Non-Commissioned Officer. Guards Équipage, 1834-1843.
843. Company-Grade Officer. Guards Équipage, 1835-1843.
844. Field-Grade Officer. Guards Équipage, 1843-1844.
845. Drum Major. Guards Équipage, 1843-1844.
846. Company-Grade Officer. Guards Équipage, 1844-1855.
847. Shako for Guards Équipage lower ranks, established 9 September 1844.
848. Company-Grade Officer and Musician. Guards Équipage, 1844-1855.
849. Field-Grade Officer, Guards Équipage Artillery Command, and Private, Guards Barge Company. 1844-1855.
850. Officer's shako, Guards Équipage, since 1845.
851. Field-Grade Officer. Guards Équipage, 1852-1855.
852. Private and Drummer. Instructional Carabinier Regiment, 1826.
853. Company-Grade Officer and NCO. Instructional Carabinier Regiment, 1826.
854. Company-Grade Officer. Instructional Carabinier Regiment, 1826.
855. Privates and Field-Grade Officer. Instructional Carabinier Regiments, 1826-1830.
856. Non-Commissioned Officer. Instructional Carabinier Regiments, 1828-1833.
857. Clerk and Craftsman. Instructional Carabinier Regiments, 1828-1844.
858. Company-Grade Officer and NCO. Instructional Carabinier Regiments, 1833.
859. Hornist and Company-Grade Officer. Instructional Carabinier Regiments, 1833-1843.
860. Private. Instructional Carabinier Regiments, 1833-1843.
861. Non-Commissioned Officer. Instructional Carabinier Regiments, 1834-1843.
862. Drummer. Instructional Carabinier Regiments, 1843-1844.
863. Private and Musician. Instructional Carabinier Regiments, 1844-1855.
864. Field-Grade Officer. Instructional Carabinier Regiments, 1845-1849.
865. Private and Company-Grade Officer. Instructional Cavalry Squadron, 1826.
866. Company-Grade Officer and Trumpeter. Instructional Cavalry Squadron, 1827.
867. NCO and Company-Grade Officer. Instructional Cavalry Squadron, 1828.
868. Private. Instructional Cavalry Squadron, 1828-1830.
869. Private. Instructional Cavalry Squadron, 1833-1841.
870. Private. Instructional Cavalry Squadron, 1834-1841.
871. Trumpeter. Instructional Cavalry Squadron, 1836-1841.
872. Private. Instructional Cavalry Squadron, 1841-1843.
873. Company-Grade Officer. Instructional Cavalry Squadron, 1843-1844.
874. Company-Grade Officer and Trumpeter. Instructional Cavalry Squadron, 1844-1855.
875. Cannoneer [*Kanonir*, i.e. private] and Company-Grade Officer. Instructional Artillery Brigade, 1826-1828.
876. Field-Grade Officers and Drummer. Instructional Artillery Brigade, 1826-1828.
877. Non-Commissioned Officer Artificer [*Feierverker*]. Instructional Artillery Brigade, 1828-1833.
878. Company-Grade Officer. Instructional Artillery Brigade, 1830-1833.
879. Bombardier [*Bombardir*, i.e. corporal]. Instructional Artillery Brigade, 1833.
880. Company-Grade Officer. Instructional Artillery Brigade, 1833.
881. Non-Commissioned Officer Artificer and Drummer. Instructional Artillery Brigade, 1834-1843.
882. Field-Grade Officer. Instructional Artillery Brigade, 1843-1844.
883. Company-Grade Officer and Cannoneer. Instructional Artillery Brigade, 1844-1855.
884. Company-Grade Officer and Private. Instructional Sapper Battalion, 1826-1828.
885. Field-Grade Officer. Instructional Sapper Battalion, 1826-1828.
886. Company-Grade Officer and NCO. Instructional Sapper Battalion, 1828-1833.
887. Private. Instructional Sapper Battalion, 1833.
888. Hornist. Instructional Sapper Battalion, 1833-1843.
889. Musician and Private. Instructional Sapper Battalion, 1834-1843.
890. Company-Grade Officer. Instructional Sapper Battalion, 1835-1843.
891. Drum Major. Instructional Sapper Battalion, 1843-1844.

Non-Commissioned Officer and Company-Grade Officer. L.-Gds. Sapper Battalion, 1826-1828.

Adjutant. L.-Gds. Sapper Battalion, 1826-1828.

798

Hornist and Company-Grade Officer. L.-Gds. Sapper Battalion, 1828-1833.

799

Company-Grade Officer. L.-Gds. Sapper Battalion, 1833.

800

Drummer. L.-Gds. Sapper Battalion, 1834-43.

801

Non-Commissioned Officer. L.-Gds. Sapper Battalion, 1834-1843.

802

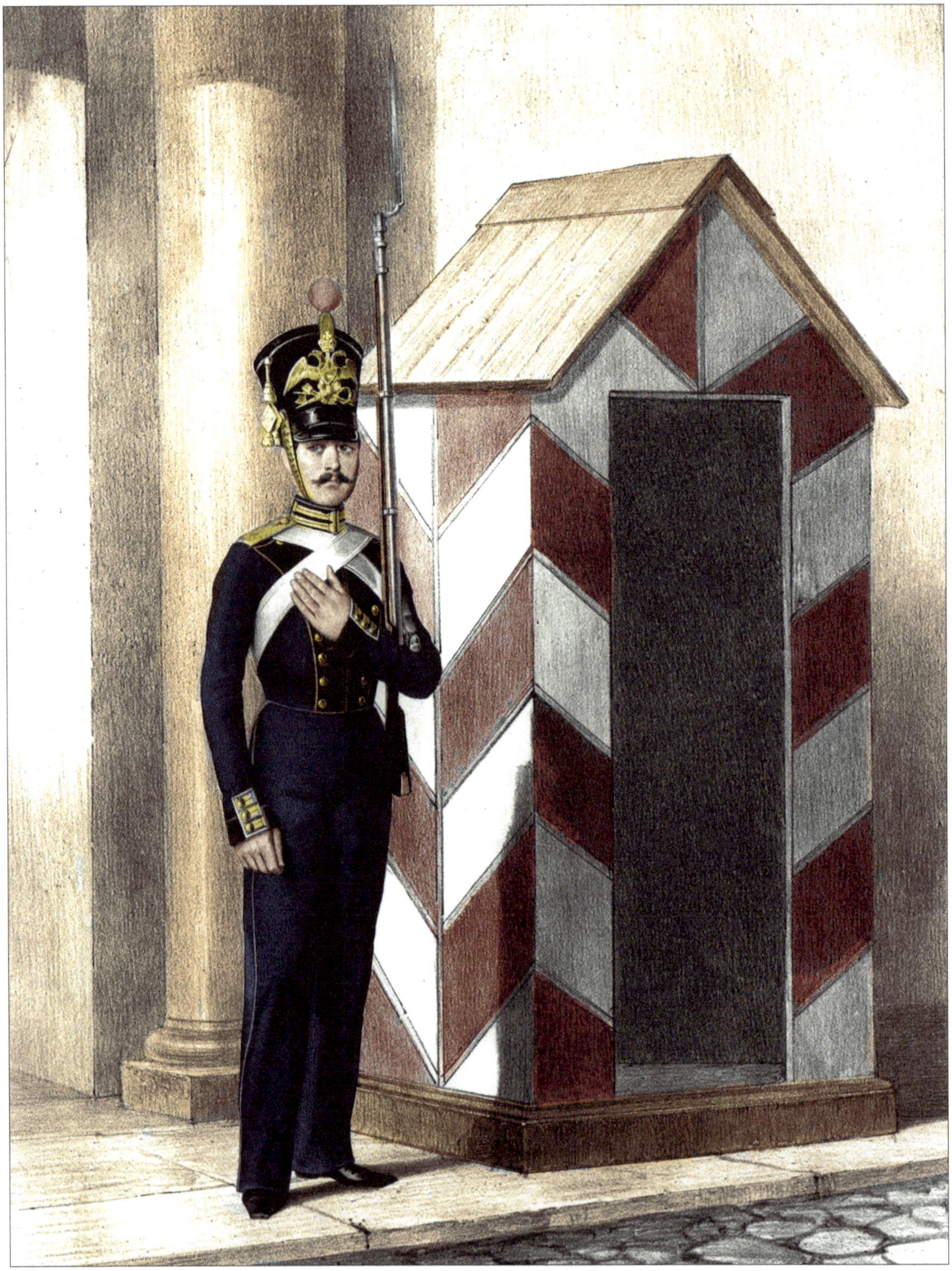

Private. L.-Gds. Sapper Battalion, 1843-1844.

803

Non-Commissioned Officer and Musician. L.-Gds. Sapper Battalion, 1844-1849.

804

Company-Grade Officer. L.-Gds. Sapper Battalion, 1845-1849.

805

Non-Commissioned Officer. L.-Gds. Horse-Pioneer Squadron, 1827-1829.

Non-Commissioned Officer and Company-Grade Officer. L.-Gds. Horse-Pioneer Squadron, 1829-1841.

Trumpeter. L.-Gds. Horse-Pioneer Squadron, 1841-1843.

Trumpeter and Field-Grade Officer. L.-Gds. Horse-Pioneer Squadron, 1843-1849.

809

Field-Grade Officer. L.-Gds. Horse-Pioneer Battalion, 1845-1849.

Private. L.-Gds. Horse-Pioneer Battalion, 1846-1855.

811

Company-Grade Officer. Guards Engineers, 1826-1846.

812

Field-Grade Officer. Guards Engineers, 1826-1846.

813

Field-Grade Officer. Guards Engineers, 1846-1849.

Field-Grade Officer. Guards General Staff, 1826-1844.

815

Company-Grade Officer. Guards General Staff, 1826-1844.

816

Generals. Guards General Staff, 1844.

817

Field-Grade Officer. Guards General Staff, 1845-1849.

818

Company-Grade Officer. Guards General Staff, 1849-1855.

Non-Commissioned Officer and Private. L.-Gds. Garrison Battalion, 1826-1828.

820

Company-Grade Officer. L.-Gds. Garrison Battalion, 1826-1828.

821

Drummer and Field-Grade Officer L.-Gds. Garrison Battalion, 1826-1828.

Drummer and Company-Grade Officer. L.-Gds. Garrison Battalion, 1828-1833.

823

Non-Commissioned Officer. L.-Gds. Garrison Battalion, 1833-1843.

824

Company-Grade Officer. L.-Gds. Garrison Battalion, 1833-1843.

Private. L.-Gds. Garrison Battalion, 1834-1843.

826

Musician and Non-Commissioned Officer. L.-Gds. Garrison Battalion, 1844-1849.

827

Company-Grade Officer and Private. Guards Invalid Companies, 1826-1828.

Non-Commissioned Officer. Guards Invalid Companies, 1828-1833.

Private. Guards Invalid No. 16 Company, 1832-1833.

830

Non-Commissioned Officer. Guards Invalid No. 16 Company, 1833-1838.

831

Private. Guards Invalid Companies, 1833-1843.

832

Company-Grade Officer. Guards Invalid Companies, 1843-1844.

Private. Guards Invalid Companies, 1844-1845.

834

Company-Grade Officer. Guards Invalid Companies, 1845-1849.

835. Private, Guards Équipage. Cannoneer, Guards Équipage Artillery Command. Non-Commissioned Officer, Guards Barge Company. 1826-1828.

Company-Grade Officers. Guards Équipage and its Artillery Command, 1826-1828.

Company-Grade Officers. Guards Barge Company, 1827-1828.

Bombardier and Company-Grade Officer. Guards Équipage Artillery Company, 1828-1830.

Drummer, Guards Équipage, and Private, Guards Barge Company. 1828-1830.

840

Clerk. Guards Équipage, 1828-1830.

Company-Grade Officer. Guards Barge Company, 1830-1843.

Non-Commissioned Officer, Guards Équipage, 1834-1843.

843

Company-Grade Officer. Guards Équipage, 1835-1843.

844

Field-Grade Officer. Guards Équipage, 1843-1844.

845

Drum Major. Guards Équipage, 1843-1844.

846

Company-Grade Officer. Guards Équipage, 1844-1855.

847

Shako for Guards Équipage lower ranks, established 9 September 1844.

Company-Grade Officer and Musician. Guards Équipage, 1844-1855.

Field-Grade Officer, Guards Équipage Artillery Command, and Private, Guards Barge Company. 1844-1855.

850

Officer's shako, Guards Équipage, since 1845.

851

Field-Grade Officer. Guards Équipage, 1852-1855.

852

Private and Drummer. Instructional Carabinier Regiment, 1826.

853

Company-Grade Officer and Non-Commissioned Officer. Instructional Carabinier Regiment, 1826.

854

Company-Grade Officer. Instructional Carabinier Regiment, 1826.

Privates and Field-Grade Officer. Instructional Carabinier Regiments, 1826-1830.

856

Non-Commissioned Officer. Instructional Carabinier Regiments, 1828-1833.

Clerk and Craftsman. Instructional Carabinier Regiments, 1828-1844.

858

Company-Grade Officer and Non-Commissioned Officer. Instructional Carabinier Regiments, 1833.

859

Hornist and Company-Grade Officer. Instructional Carabinier Regiments, 1833-1843.

860

Private. Instructional Carabinier Regiments, 1833-1843.

861

Non-Commissioned Officer. Instructional Carabinier Regiments, 1834-1843.

862

Drummer. Instructional Carabinier Regiments, 1843-1844.

863

Private and Musician. Instructional Carabinier Regiments, 1844-1855.

864

Field-Grade Officer. Instructional Carabinier Regiments, 1845-1849.

Private and Company-Grade Officer. Instructional Cavalry Squadron, 1826.

Company-Grade Officer and Trumpeter. Instructional Cavalry Squadron, 1827.

Non-Commissioned Officer and Company-Grade Officer. Instructional Cavalry Squadron, 1828.

868

Private. Instructional Cavalry Squadron, 1828-1830.

Private. Instructional Cavalry Squadron, 1833-1841.

Private. Instructional Cavalry Squadron, 1834-1841.

871

Trumpeter. Instructional Cavalry Squadron, 1836-1841.

872

Private. Instructional Cavalry Squadron, 1841-1843.

873

Company-Grade Officer. Instructional Cavalry Squadron, 1843-1844.

874

Company-Grade Officer and Trumpeter. Instructional Cavalry Squadron, 1844-1855.

875

Cannoneer [Kanonir, i.e. private] and Company-Grade Officer. Instructional Artillery Brigade, 1826-1828.

876

Field-Grade Officers and Drummer. Instructional Artillery Brigade, 1826-1828.

877

Non-Commissioned Officer Artificer [Feierverker]. Instructional Artillery Brigade, 1828-1833.

878

Company-Grade Officer. Instructional Artillery Brigade, 1830-1833.

Bombardier [Bombardir, i.e. corporal]. Instructional Artillery Brigade, 1833.

880

Company-Grade Officer. Instructional Artillery Brigade, 1833.

881

Non-Commissioned Officer Artificer and Drummer. Instructional Artillery Brigade, 1834-1843.

882

Field-Grade Officer. Instructional Artillery Brigade, 1843-1844.

883

Company-Grade Officer and Cannoneer. Instructional Artillery Brigade, 1844-1855.

Company-Grade Officer and Private. Instructional Sapper Battalion, 1826-1828.

885

Field-Grade Officer. Instructional Sapper Battalion, 1826-1828.

886

Company-Grade Officer and Non-Commissioned Officer. Instructional Sapper Battalion, 1828-1833.

887

Private. Instructional Sapper Battalion, 1833.

888

Hornist. Instructional Sapper Battalion, 1833-1843.

Musician and Private. Instructional Sapper Battalion, 1834-1843.

890

Company-Grade Officer. Instructional Sapper Battalion, 1835-1843.

Drum Major. Instructional Sapper Battalion, 1843-1844.

SOLDIERS, WEAPONS & UNIFORMS ALREADY PUBLISHED
(SOME TITLES)

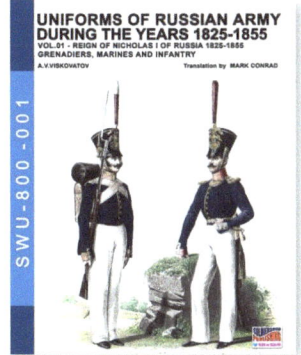
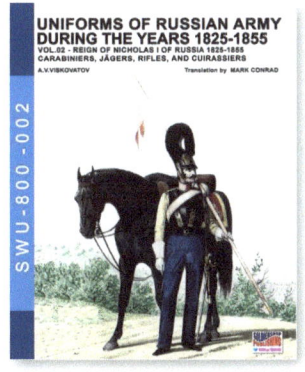
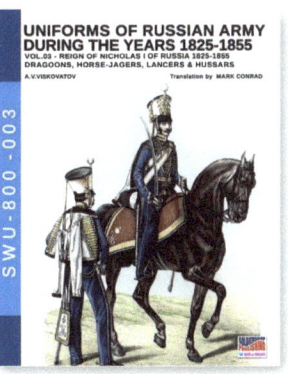
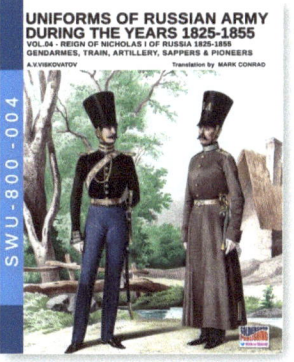
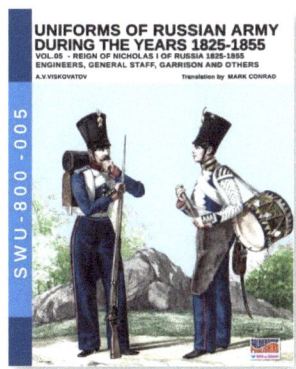
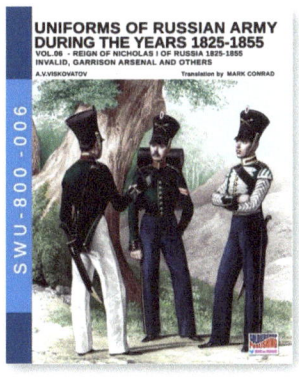
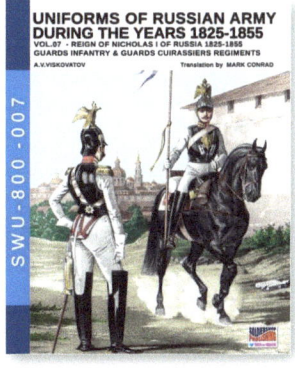

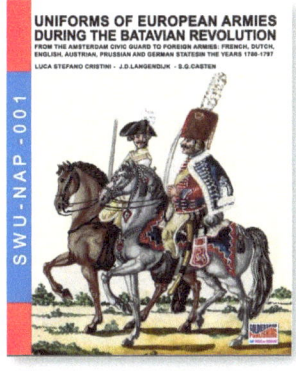

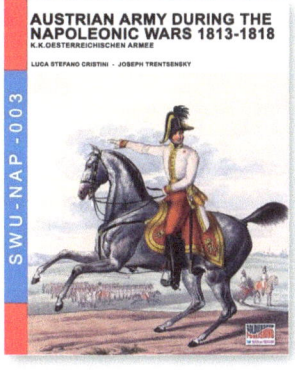
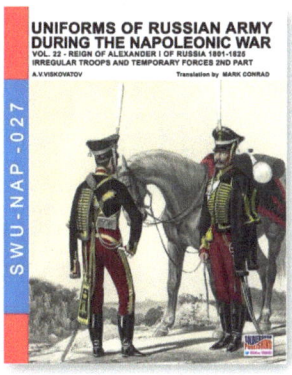
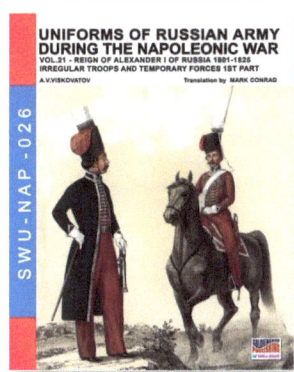
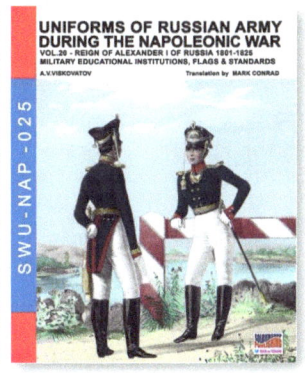
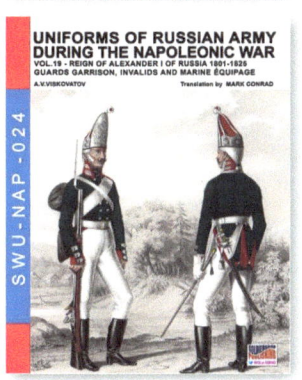
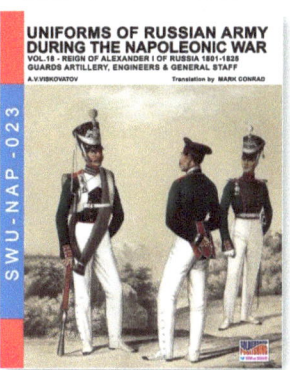